Pick Up the Pieces
A Survivor's Story
of Life with Ray Wyre

Charmaine Richardson

❦ WATERSIDE PRESS

Pick Up the Pieces
A Survivor's Story of Life with Ray Wyre
Charmaine Richardson

ISBN 978-1-909976-63-4 (Paperback)
ISBN 978-1-910979-67-9 (Epub ebook)
ISBN 978-1-910979-68-6 (Adobe ebook)

Copyright © 2018 This work is the copyright of Charmaine Richardson. All intellectual property and associated rights are hereby asserted and reserved by the author in full compliance with UK, European and international law. No part of this book may be copied, reproduced, stored in any retrieval system or transmitted in any form or by any means, including in hard copy or via the internet, without the prior written permission of the publishers to whom all such rights have been assigned worldwide.

Cover design © 2018 Waterside Press by www.gibgob.com

Printed by Lightning Source.

Main UK distributor Gardners Books, 1 Whittle Drive, Eastbourne, East Sussex, BN23 6QH. Tel: +44 (0)1323 521777; sales@gardners.com; www.gardners.com

North American distribution Ingram Book Company, One Ingram Blvd, La Vergne, TN 37086, USA. Tel: (+1) 615 793 5000; inquiry@ingramcontent.com

Cataloguing-In-Publication Data A catalogue record for this book can be obtained from the British Library.

e-book *Pick Up the Pieces* is available as an ebook and also to subscribers of Ebrary, Ebsco, Myilibrary and Dawsonera.

Published 2018 by
Waterside Press Ltd
Sherfield Gables
Sherfield on Loddon, Hook
Hampshire RG27 0JG.

Telephone +44(0)1256 882250
Online catalogue WatersidePress.co.uk
Email enquiries@watersidepress.co.uk

Table of Contents

About the author *v*
Acknowledgements *vi*
Encomium *vii*
Dedication *ix*

    Introduction 13

1 **The Meeting** 17

2 **Once Upon a Time Bomb** 21

3 **The Fall of Utopia** 27
        Aspects of Sexual Abuse *35*

4 **Silly Me!** 37

5 **'Hello Sailor'** 51
        The Role of the Dice *53*

6 **Moving On** 55

7 **Ray and Me** 59

8 **Language and Feeling Uncomfortable** 71

9 **Unpacking *The Murder of Childhood*** 75
        Black's History *78*
        Key Pointers *87*

10 **Farewell to Gracewell: Goodbye Common Sense** 89
        The Two-way Mirror   *91*
        De-frocked Priests and Other Distortions   *94*
        Survival   *96*
        Abused Abusers, Red-herrings and Listening to Voices   *99*
        Martin   *100*

11 **Jane and Maureen** 103
        Jane: 'Do I Qualify to Join this Group?'   *103*
        Maureen: Finding Solace   *106*

12 **Mind Your Language!** 109
        Behavioural Insights   *119*
        Other Work on Positive Conditioning   *120*
        When Methods Fail   *121*
        Familiarity   *124*
        Analysis of Black's Dialogue   *126*

Epilogue   *129*
        'Goodnight, Sweetheart'   *130*
        Picking Up the Pieces   *132*
        How Am I Doing Nowadays?   *135*

Recommended reading   *137*

Index   *138*

About the author

Charmaine Richardson grew up in Ealing, the second of four children, before moving to Watford where she attended St Michael's Roman Catholic Senior School, then a secretarial course at Casio College. Her first marriage, aged 22, produced two children. In 1986, after a bout of depression she sought counselling for sexual abuse experienced during childhood. She went on to set up a self-help group, subsequently joining Luton Rape Crisis Centre. She obtained a degree in English Literature at Northampton University as a mature student and has since pursued a variety of careers: counselling, home tutoring and funeral celebrant. She met and married the noted sex-offender expert Ray Wyre in the late-1990s and her life with him forms a central part of this book. She also contributed to the 2nd edition of Ray's book with journalist Tim Tate, *The Murder of Childhood* (2018).[1] Nowadays she runs a group for women abused in childhood at a local medical centre when not 'visiting tea-rooms with friends and spoiling her grandchildren'.

---

1. Waterside Press (2018). In this book *The Murder of Childhood* is often abbreviated to *MoC*.

Acknowledgements

I would like to thank friends and family who supported and encouraged me during the writing of this book. Ben, Richard, Jeannie, Ron Lacey, Amanda Vernalls and many others. I particularly thank, with all my heart, Amber whose patience and interest kept me going. Her responses and comments each step of the way have always been positive and constructive.

In writing the book I have also (and finally) fulfilled my mother's wish — that I should write a book! Sadly, Mum is no longer with us to witness her wish coming to fruition — and, in spite of *Pick Up the Pieces* revealing some of the shortcomings of motherhood, I'm sure she would have approved.

I would also like to remember my dear friend and colleague Hazel Pedder.

However, I doubt this book would have seen the light of day had it not been for Rik and David of Monster Films who introduced me to Bryan Gibson my publisher. Many thanks.

This book was written with some little people in mind — my grandchildren. But also all little people whose safety and autonomy it is our duty to protect.

Charmaine Richardson
July 2018

Encomium

Ray Wyre was simultaneously a perpetual inspiration and a regular nightmare. I was immensely privileged to work with him for 20 years, making films and writing books about the problems of paedophilia and child sexual abuse. Over those two decades I witnessed first hand his groundbreaking technique with offenders and saw the extraordinary change it could bring about in men who had often abused children for many years.

We also campaigned together, trying to inform public opinion and to push successive Governments to see the vital importance of protecting children. They key to this was—and remains—understanding not just how paedophiles target their victims, but what drives them to do so. In both of these areas, Ray was simply pre-eminent.

And he was tireless, tramping from one interview to the next, always calm, always making the case that paedophilia and child sexual abuse are problems far too prevalent and damaging to be ignored or belittled. I saluted his stamina, just as I marvelled at his patience and persistence. I learned from Ray every day we worked together.

And the nightmare? Outside his professional life Ray was the most chaotically disorganized man I have ever met. I lost count of the number of occasions when he left his wallet, car keys or Filofax in curry houses, restaurants and conference centres, requiring us regularly to re-trace our steps in the hope of re-uniting him with them.

One of the many strengths of Charmaine's touching memoir of life with Ray is that she gives us an insight into what made this extraordinary, vital crusader on behalf of children tick, enabling us to see the fuller picture of the man as well as the expert. Had Ray lived to read it he would, I am sure, have broken into that cheeky, childlike grin, ruefully acknowledging his faults before cheerfully encouraging us back into the struggle.

Because he knew it is a struggle. The debate over how best to investigate child sexual abuse, and how to protect children from those who would abuse them, is dangerously polarised; as Charmaine explains, too often politicians and the public alike reach for seemingly-simple, knee-jerk 'solutions' to a complex series of interlinked issues or, just as fatally, seek to deny the vast scale of the problem.

Ray took every opportunity to counter this divided and angry argument with quiet, evidence-based reason. Just as he did in sessions with offenders, he used language which managed to lower the temperature whilst never taking a backward step. Charmaine's stress on the importance of the words we choose, and how we use them, would — I know — have delighted him.

Saluté, then, Ray Wyre: doughty warrior on behalf of the protection of children, and my mentor and inspiration in the never-ending battle. I — and the world — miss his presence and his constant encouragement to keep fighting on behalf of those who are too small to do so themselves. But saluté, also, to Charmaine: this book both keeps the banner flying and helps us see the human man behind the paramount professional.

Tim Tate
June 2018

This book is dedicated to Jack, Henry, Beau,
Darcie, Berry, Eden and Adam.

Ray Wyre

Introduction

It was at a conference in Hemel Hempstead that I first set eyes on Ray Wyre. I'd been invited to hear him speak before — but declined. He was in the middle of setting up the Gracewell Clinic in Birmingham and was being described as a pioneer — a maverick, a revolutionary, etc. working with men who sexually abuse.

'Why,' I asked myself, 'would I want to listen to an apologist for sex-offenders?' At that point in my life I wanted all sex-offenders to be castrated from the neck down. So, no thank you, I didn't want to go. A talk by Michelle Elliot on the work of Kidscape some time later was a different matter. Mr Wyre had been tacked on at the end — I could handle that, I thought.

How was I to know my life was about to change seismically during his one hour presentation — and that this unassuming man in his grey suit, white shirt and red tie, who held his audience spellbound, would one day become my husband?

But now, standing on the podium, this cuddly, poor Roy Orbison lookalike, was coming out with stuff I'd never heard before. It was embarrassing because he was telling *my* story. Had he met my warped grandfather? He must have. Not only was he talking *about* me — he was talking *to* me. I felt conspicuous as though he knew personal information about me and was sharing it with everybody else in the room. He didn't know me, of course; he didn't know my story, but he knew exactly how my grandfather had targeted, groomed and abused me — and now *my* secret was out. Whether it was his charisma or his impressive knowledge of abusive behaviour that bowled me over I'm not entirely sure. But bowled over I was.

A few months before, I had been granted use of the Bury Mill Family Centre to run a self-help group for women who had been abused in childhood. Having 'been there' myself and, after having some counselling,

I decided that setting-up such a group would be the next step. I had literally walked into social services one morning and told a social worker what my intention was. It was the right time for talking about abuse as everyone wanted to be seen to be addressing the issue. The social worker took my details. Within the week, John Horsfield, Head of Social Services, contacted me. Within the month I'd got the okay to set up a group under the auspices of the National Society for the Prevention of Cruelty to Children (NSPCC). Two months later following a lead article in the local press, the first group meeting took place at Bury Mill.

This book is about my own personal voyage from childhood to now and the man I met along the way who had a colossal effect on my life in every respect: Ray Wyre. I will refer to my own experience of abuse merely to demonstrate the effects of sexual abuse. It is also about unpacking Ray's enormously important book *The Murder of Childhood* (*MoC*) which contains his interviews with the multiple child-murderer Robert Black and what Ray learned from him.

Written in 1995, *MoC* was ahead of its time. Over two decades on and it's *still* ahead of its time. This speaks volumes for the book, but does not reflect well on our progress in making the world a safer place for our children — and grandchildren. *MoC* challenges bigotry and dares to suggest that, in ignoring abusers, we are complicit in sexual child-abuse. With insight and belief in Ray's work, I am delighted that it is now being republished. I would like to draw on it to show how we can learn how to protect our children better.

Furthermore, I believe that in order to do this we must look at how we condition children through our use of language. The language we use with them can play a vital role in increasing their safety and decreasing risk. So, I hope this book will at least prompt discussion on the way we speak to children and the effect our words can have on them — even if you don't agree with it!

Of course the latest threat to child safety is the internet — a medium which cannot be monitored adequately. It is an abuser's dream. The anonymity afforded by chatrooms and the like makes it a hundred times easier for offenders to abuse from the comfort of their own homes. And as we are nowhere near beginning to improve child safety and we continue to bury our heads in the sand by refusing to listen to how perpetrators operate, then when it comes to social media, sex-offenders are way, way ahead of us and continue to gain ground. But some of the things I say in this book, particularly about listening to children and whether they feel that they can tell their parents when they feel uncomfortable about something are as relevant here as they are to other methods of child abuse.

After several false starts I am now at the most peaceful time in my life and have finally grown into the rest of me. With an increasing number of grandchildren in my life the message of child protection has become more urgent and closer to my heart.

Pick Up the Pieces

CHAPTER 1

The Meeting

Nineteen-eighty-eight the Pavilion, Hemel Hempstead and I have just been embarrassed by a talk by Ray Wyre, pioneer of the Gracewell Clinic for sex-offenders.

In a bold move for any practitioner at any time, Ray, along with his main collaborator Trevor Price, founded the completely independent Gracewell Clinic in Birmingham in 1988, with the help of a small number of colleagues and limited financial backing. It was the first residential clinic in Britain for sex-offenders and it accepted 'referrals' for assessment and preventative work, initially from a growing number of the local Probation Services that then existed in England and Wales. Gracewell later and in addition came to be seen as a facility that could serve as a more promising alternative to existing criminal processes.

Amongst many ground-breaking innovations, Ray used 'seasoned' offenders at Gracewell—those familiar with techniques for avoiding responsibility, minimising harm, normalising sexual and predatory misconduct and blaming victims—to challenge and confront the beliefs, lies, denials and evasions of new arrivals. The knowledge he and fellow practitioners acquired through this work became an important source of information for police investigators, criminal psychologists, the courts and others from across the UK and abroad.

As explained in *Chapter 10*, the clinic closed in 1993, in part due to a short-sighted 'not in my backyard' attitude to paedophiles, who consequently, once the work stopped, became freer to prey on communities. In 2002, a similar fate befell Gracewell's successor, the Wolvercote Clinic in Surrey. Despite Ray's trailblazing work, there is now no residential unit of this kind in the UK and the specialist work that he began to encourage, understand and prevent the secretive targeting and grooming of children has, I believe, been largely at a standstill.

Ray's presentation to us that day took place towards the start of this independent venture. We broke for coffee and everyone descended on him. I wanted to follow suit but didn't feel confident enough. When the crowd cleared he headed towards me. Towards the coffee pot and biscuits, actually. I wanted to run-off and stay put at the same time. My feet decided for me and I stood stock still. He said something and I bumbled something and that was it. I was both relieved and disappointed when he moved away to talk to someone who had something coherent to say.

After our awkward first meeting, I noticed that this man Wyre was never off the telly. He was on talk shows, discussion panels, the news and he even infiltrated the radio. He dominated the airwaves. Nowhere was a Ray-free zone. However, what he had to say was a real eye-opener: Abusers enjoy abusing; castrating them is futile and makes them more dangerous; women should be able to dress as they like without feeling threatened; monsters don't get close to children — nice men do. I'd never heard such common sense before. In his soft, gentle manner he took on the Establishment and wouldn't back down. Then fate took a hand and put us both on a collision course.

On one of my visits to the NSPCC, I pulled into the car park just as a silver Saab zoomed in and took the last space. Cheeky! I parked blocking someone in and got out. Heading towards the door I noticed the Saab driver emerge and head in the same direction. It was Ray. He opened the door for me and we went in together. Embarrassment overtook me and we sat in the waiting room — me tongue-tied, again. Ray then proceeded to tell me all about this new clinic for sex-offenders which he was involved in setting-up. On and on he went expounding the virtues and benefits of Gracewell. There had never been anything like it before and he was so excited.

His enthusiasm was infectious. For sure it was going to be an enormous success. But I just really wanted him to go now, because I felt certain he would be expecting an intelligent response. And I didn't have one. Then he mentioned that he needed someone from a survivor group to appear on telly with him to discuss Gracewell and—could he have my number? I wasn't sure—but couldn't refuse. With that, he was gone.

The long, painful journey to this waiting room, however, had begun many years before, in Ealing. My life then was pretty much uneventful. Ordinary—dull in fact. In every family, each member will have a different tale to tell—a totally different point of view of a shared event. So, this account is about my experience alone and is not a judgement or criticism of anyone. It does not in any way set out to undermine anyone else's experiences or opinions. And it is not a form of navel-gazing literary therapy. These are my views, my perspective and my opinions.

Pick Up the Pieces

CHAPTER 2

Once Upon a Time Bomb

We lived at 19 Amherst Road—that's mum Mary, dad Joe, older brother Christopher and me. Dad worked at Ultra Radios and Televisions as an engineer, mum had been a secretary but now had her hands full with me. Apparently, on seeing me for the first time, Christopher declared, 'No! Not this one. I want a bigger one!' and stomped off in bitter disappointment. The little playmate his parents had been promising for nigh on nine months was not fit for purpose. But I was forgiven. He even forgave me when six years later I sat on his hamster and squashed its face to mulch.

We were happy in our little family. Unhappiness for us meant not being able to stay up after seven or not having the last doughnut. It was during this bliss that my world suffered an earthquake and spun off its axis. I don't know whether living in a relative utopia made what happened more of a shock or not but the utter unexpectedness of it resonated throughout my life.

Christopher and I were brought up to be obedient, polite and respectful, especially towards adults and particularly senior family members. I wouldn't have known how to have a temper tantrum or answer back. We were controlled from within. Children had to *know their place*, they must be *seen and not heard*. If ever there was a cliché to destroy childhood it was the latter.

Life was expected, predictable—there were no nasty surprises. The routine was reassuring. I didn't know it at the time but it was sort of idyllic. Being fifties' children we had the best of everything. We were the post-war, much-wanted generation. Free orange-juice, malt, cod-liver oil, Bengers, all disgusting but good for us. There were regular school medicals, a proper cooked school lunch, free school milk and the Nit Lady. Nothing it would seem, was too much for us. Bliss.

If we were bad or noisy or broke a jade vase in the sitting-room on Sunday we got smacked. But more than that. Smacking I could deal with. It never hurt anyway and you knew where you stood with smacking — job done. No, it was something else — a different technique, there were tacit rules hidden in our upbringing and re-affirmed by our fifties' world. In fact, I don't remember mum ever raising her voice. Being 'good' obedient children was what we had to aspire to. Teachers, our parents' friends, television, books, radio — the message was omnipresent. It was in the walls, ceilings, floors and sky of our world. The ideal boy would help dad repair the car, do carpentry and decorate the house. The ideal girl would help mum in the kitchen, sew and arrange flowers. The Ladybird books were *us*.

Numerous trips to Casualty around this time would suggest that I was a little too lively. The first was when I hung on the door knob and sprained my arm resulting in my having to wear a sling. The second was when I decided to somersault off the top bunk expecting to land on my feet instead of my face on an unlit paraffin heater. I split my chin so badly that mum had to dial 999. Eight stitches and 60 years later I still have the scar to prove it. I'm grateful for it now as it is a much requested story for the grandchildren. They especially like the ambulance *ringing* its bell.

Another time my brother accidently dropped a log on my foot. No-one realised it was fractured until after we'd walked round Kew Gardens for a few hours and my foot had swelled to twice its size. My moaning and crying throughout this visit was met with, 'Come on now, stop making a fuss. I can't carry you anymore. You're too heavy. And stop pestering Uncle Ian to carry you. It's not polite to keep asking'.

The next day Casualty revealed my foot to be fractured and needed a plaster-cast which I sported for six weeks. Although not deliberately neglectful, by ignoring my pleas the underlying message was, 'We don't believe you. Stop making a fuss. Your version of reality is wrong. We know better'. Even though my moaning was justified it was more a case of, 'All sorted now. Hush.' That's just how it was in those days. Children accepted they were more often than not in the wrong.

Our home was always spick and span. Once we'd got a telly I abandoned my toys in favour of *Watch with Mother, Picture Book, Andy Pandy* and the eloquent *Bill and Ben*. Christopher was irritatingly creative and could draw beautifully. He asked me to sit for him once whilst he sketched my portrait. After what seemed like ages he showed me his masterpiece. A horse. Yes, he could draw beautifully, but only horses.

Up to the age of seven I learned: I had to be obedient; I had to respect all grown-ups (especially family members); I must be polite to everyone; it was my duty to be kind and put others first; I must behave like a young lady; I mustn't make a fuss; I must always tell the truth and, last but not least, for some strange reason only known to some adults, I had to kiss every visiting grown-up who came through the door. It seemed to work because every time I did this it evoked an, 'Ahh, isn't she lovely' from the recipient. I never liked doing it—it felt odd. Commercial TV was the favoured channel and, although its adverts were not specifically aimed at children, when children did appear they were in stereotypical roles. The advert for washing-up liquid springs to mind: a little girl helping mummy wash the dishes—and enjoying it.

My personal experience of my father was that he was distant. He didn't know how to be with me and I interpreted this to mean that he was a bit disappointed. There were just little things along the way that I picked-up on. Subtle nuances which hinted that there was something about being a girl and something about being me that didn't quite pass muster. It felt that I lacked more than a penis. Being a girl meant not being the best.

When I helped mum in the kitchen, I discovered that I was a 'good girl'. When I did 'girly' things I suddenly became accepted and acceptable. Climbing trees and whistling prompted my brother to tell on me, 'Girls aren't allowed to whistle!' Why?

It is interesting how the subliminal messages can be the more powerful. They just creep in without us even knowing it is happening—moulding and sculpting away year-after-year. It's the constancy that reifies them. Being a girl meant being second-class.

Having come to the conclusion, over my four years in the world, that I was never going to get any closer to dad, I developed an attachment to a family friend. Uncle Willie always swept me up in his arms and greeted me as if he was delighted to see me. I loved it. I loved him. I felt comfortable with him and he didn't mind me being me. It was a lovely relationship. Until the day I blew it. Whilst he and dad were hunched-over looking in the back of a TV set, I pirouetted over, hugged the back of Uncle Willie and declared, 'I wish *you* were my daddy!'

Boy, the flack I got for that was unbelievable. Later that evening my dad asked me in a grave self-pitying tone, 'So, you don't love your father, eh?' I didn't know how to answer. Should I appease him and say, 'Oh daddy, no-one could ever take your place. No one ignores me quite the way you do. You're the best.' Or say, 'Actually no. I don't know what I'm supposed to feel towards you. I'm only four, you see, and don't have the vocabulary or confidence to express articulately what I really think and feel about you. You're supposed to be the grown-up here.' Instead, I absorbed it as another one of *my* failures.

Another example that stands out in my memory is the time Sadie came to stay. Sadie was the four-year-old daughter of my mum's friend, Joan. Joan had to go into hospital and her husband was working abroad. So Sadie came to stay with us for a few days and things got off to a bad start. Sadie was to sleep in *my* room, in *my* bed and use *my* Noddy cup and plate. It was Goldilocks in real time. What's more, her presence turned my dad into Coco the bloody clown. He couldn't do enough to make her feel 'at home'. She was allowed to play with my toys — and not put them away, leave food on her (my) plate and was not even told off for picking her nose and wiping it on the wall. Double standards or what? Dad in his infinite wisdom told me to stop being selfish and let her play with my Popeye doll. It wasn't Sadie's fault and I actually liked her. But Sadie had to go.

The next day I thought I'd take her to 'find her mum'. We went out of the front gate, I even allowed her to push my doll's pram. Off we started down the road and I reassured her that it was all right for her to cross the road on her own. 'I'll wait here for you'. At that moment I heard my mother's shriek of 'Stop!' echo down the road. Sadie, unfortunately, stopped. With my murderous plan thwarted, I explained that Sadie was missing her mum and I was just taking her to see her. No-one ever found out the truth. The most painful part of Sadie's stay was that

I realised my dad could be all the things I wanted him to be. He just couldn't be like that with me.

Christopher and I went to St. Gregory's Catholic School in Woodfield Road. As schools went this was the business. Strict uniforms, polished parquet floors, an immense library and a wonderful headmaster, Mr Macaffrey. Just a shame I didn't want to go. I loved hanging around with mum.

One morning father was asked to take me to school. This had never happened before and I have to admit to being excited. Now he was going to have to hold my hand and listen as I talked to him. I promised myself I wouldn't wriggle my hand when he held it because that used to annoy him. As we opened the front-door, however, he put on his crash helmet and gauntlets. Wow—I was going to go on his motorbike! Then I'd be really close to him, I erroneously thought. He proceeded to get on his bike saying to me, 'Now you walk up to that lamppost and wait. I'll ride over to you, all right?' And we continued thus until we got to school. My thoughts: of course he wouldn't want to walk with me—why would he? I'm sure there was a perfectly good explanation for this bizarre journey, but I felt silly standing there, waving him off. What was it about me? I felt I was not quite what they had expected. A great opportunity to be close with me was lost.

Early on I noticed a disparity in Christopher's and my Christmas presents. One year, whilst he got an enormous train set, I got a nurse's outfit with a stethoscope that had been *Made in Hong Kong*. Another year he got a Raleigh Palm Beach bike—I got a tiny toy sewing-machine that was also *Made in Hong Kong*. The only thing it sewed was my finger.

However, the following year I got a watch. That was a clear message that I'd achieved 'good girl' status. Unfortunately they forgot to give it to me until Christmas day was all but over! A very unfortunate omission. It was the typewriter that was the funniest of the lot. Instead of a working keyboard it had a *picture* of a keyboard on it! The only way you could get it to type was to move the huge wheel to the letter of each word you wanted to 'type' then press down hard on the spacebar and hope for the best. For sure the first Caxton would have been quicker. But like the fast-expanding elephant in the room, we didn't mention it.

If I'm beginning to sound ungrateful—after all there were and are children who receive nothing at all at Christmas or any other time of the year—it is not out of self-pity. I'm only trying to demonstrate how a child's self-esteem and self-worth can be corroded by negative messages even if they're not meant.

One morning my mother called us to their bedroom and gently asked whether we would like a baby sister or baby brother?' I couldn't believe it. Finally, we could be like all the other Catholic families whose mums waited at the school gates with prams overflowing with the results of Catholic rules on contraception. I was overjoyed. But this wasn't going to be a one-off.

CHAPTER 3

The Fall of Utopia

A few months later mum brought home a screaming baby brother for us to play with and all was well until... my paternal grandfather came to live with us. The bomb had moved in. Having gambled away all his money he was now penniless and homeless, so we welcomed him into our home. I was not inclined to greet him. He made me feel uncomfortable and after a while my parents were having to tell me to be polite to *Grampie*.

He often walked me to school in the mornings. On the way he began talking inappropriately about stuff I shouldn't know. Pure filth. The bomb had begun to tick. The first time it happened I boasted at school that my grandfather had brought me in. I was confused by the conversation that had just taken place so I was trying to normalise the situation — expose it to fresh air, to see what would happen. When I got home that afternoon I didn't mention anything to mum. *He* was still there in any case — as he was always going to be. I didn't go near him. I don't know what I felt, it just seemed unsafe to be anywhere close to his orbit.

His intention was not only to tell me about inappropriate stuff but to progress to showing me. The bomb exploded. The first time it happened was when he was 'looking after' me. Mum had gone shopping leaving me and my baby brother with him. I was off school with tonsillitis. I remember the shock I felt from the core of my being. I was totally unprepared. By the time my mother returned home my world had completely turned on its axis. I couldn't look her in the eye. I could never hold eye-contact with her or anyone else again for many decades after that.

My relationship with my parents deteriorated. My father became even more inaccessible as though he sensed I was different. With mum it was a question of trying even harder to be a 'good girl' because when I helped around the house — and changed nappies and did the ironing, etc. — she was very happy with me. I felt she really loved that 'good girl'. And I needed that love in order to survive.

I couldn't tell anyone what was going on because I was scared as my grandfather was highly esteemed. Also, sex was a subject not discussed in our family and we weren't given names for genitalia let alone how they worked! I had also started to feel guilty, dirty and bad. Anyhow, by the time he descended on us, hadn't I learned some valuable lessons about being a seven-year-old girl?: I had to be obedient; I had to respect all grown-ups (especially family members, including him); I must be polite to everyone; it was my duty to be kind and put others first; I must behave like a young lady; I mustn't make a fuss.

I became withdrawn. Looking back I think I was in a kind of shock. This withdrawal response was not a bad thing — it meant that, in my way, I was reacting to something in my life that was wrong. I knew it was wrong and my psyche was challenging it. I didn't just absorb it unquestioningly.

My father clearly adored his dad and listened with endless sympathy to his ramblings about how he had gambled away his gem collection, how much money he owed people, his gambling debts and his unpaid loans. In the mornings my grandfather would shuffle into the kitchen humming tunelessly. *Rambling Rose*, possibly. Every breakfast time there he was. He'd kiss me on the top of my head so everyone could see and make a snorting, phlegmy, snotty sound. I wanted to vomit.

My school work went down the drain. I couldn't concentrate — I was lost in my own thoughts. Mrs Dangerfield, my teacher, pulled me out in front of the class once and told me to stand outside in the corridor. 'Stop daydreaming child! Now get out.' Out in the corridor I looked at my face in the mirror above the washbasin. Did I still look the same? Was I still me? My eyebrows distracted me — hey, I can still make them dance separately.

A good way to describe life at the time is this: I was a child who was living outside of the safety of the womb. I should have been within the safety zone of my mother but was now cast out. I had a feeling of locked-outness. I was locked-out of my safe environment and locked-*in* to a dangerous one. It was all very strange — and this strangeness was becoming familiar because that is where I lived now. But I didn't want to live here and I didn't know how to get back. I'd lost my way. It was all a bit *Hansel and Gretal*-ish. I could see my family through this pane of glass with my grandfather in the middle, together, and I just couldn't reach them anymore. They were all on the other side of the glass. It's like this giant cuckoo had taken my place. There was a strong fear of rejection too: 'If they knew about me, they wouldn't want me.'

My tonsillitis was recurring at an alarming rate and I was admitted to hospital. I remember mum coming into my room, cradling me in her arms and whispering, 'I love you, darling'. Wow my mother still loved me — that was so reassuring to hear. Ten days later I was back home but the situation with my grandfather hadn't changed.

Nineteen-sixty-four and mum was pregnant yet again. 'Would you like a little sister or little brother?' was wearing thin. And it wasn't as if we could say, 'No thanks. We'll give it a miss.' Mum became super-busy.

I was all but pushed out now. The only person who had time for me was my grandfather. And in an incomprehensible, reprehensible way (probably only another abused person could relate to this) I had an investment in maintaining that relationship. It was the only place in my life where someone had time for me. In a distorted way I had power. There was a price to pay for this 'power', but that price was only me.

One day he said he had a wristwatch for me. Believing this gift to be above board, I boasted to everyone that Grampie was going to give me a watch. My dad learned about it and went nuts. Then he asked me in the accusatory paternal tone that parents possess, 'Is it true that you asked Grampie for a watch?' Thinking and knowing that my grandfather wouldn't back me up if I told the truth, I said, 'Yes, I did ask him for a watch' … 'But I was only joking,' I added trying to save myself. A lecture followed and I was left in no doubt that they were all disappointed in me.

I'd learned from this, though, that I could use blackmail as a way of getting something out of him. So I asked him for money to buy an inflatable canoe. There wasn't even a canal nearby. I'd seen this canoe in Woolworths for 27 shillings and sixpence and I wanted it. I boldly asked my grandfather for the money. He duly paid up. However, I had a job explaining where I got the money from so I added lies to the blackmail to clear myself: I told them I'd been saving my pocket money. I wanted to love that canoe but I couldn't. It was a dirty canoe — contaminated because it was ill-gotten — almost as if I'd stolen it. I also extracted money from him for a pair of jeans. Half-a-crown here, ten bob there. In my way I was trying to make sense of a senseless situation.

With the family expanding and dad's new job offer, we moved to Watford and although my grandfather stayed in Ealing he made many visits. The only thing that kept me going was my mother's love. I was terrified of losing that — so I'd do anything she wanted. From changing nappies to ironing and washing-up I'd try to make myself indispensable — and she appreciated it. On occasions she would leave me a 'Thank you' card which I would treasure. But I still couldn't shake off the thought that *if she really knew what was going on, she wouldn't love me.* I began to hate myself. The feeling of unworthiness was compelling.

Neither Christopher nor I took to this alien little town. It didn't feel like home. And it was a lot colder for some reason. As for the school — it felt Dickensian in every respect except discipline. Holy Rood was more *rude* than *holy* and I found it unsettling. By 1967 we were both attending St Michael's senior school in Garston. This was certainly more like we were used to. Crisp, orderly and strict. And it was awash with nuns. All very reassuring for a couple of Catholic kids.

However, I had begun to feel different from the other girls. Whilst they were into Barbie dolls, make-up and back-combing their hair, I preferred cars, guns, and guitars. I didn't want to be a girl — it was too embarrassing. I liked boys — a lot — I just didn't think they would be interested in me. I was skinny, quiet and awkward.

I noted that there were a couple of girls in the year above me to whom I was drawn. Information they inadvertently leaked was affirming in one sense because, though I didn't disclose anything about myself, I was pretty sure they were experiencing something similar in their lives. However, the way these girls dealt with it opened up a whole new world to me. They were turning it round to their benefit. I became aware of a seedy side of life that I knew I could belong to and feel comfortable in.

Promiscuity, drugs, drink—even prostitution, I suspected. This scared and interested me at the same time. Clearly these two girls had fallen victim to this life, by whom I didn't know. I know one of them became pregnant. Sex and sexual value had become a currency for them. Rather than being something enjoyed in a loving relationship, it had become a much sought-after, much-touted commodity which could be given in exchange for money or in the hope of receiving love in return. Of course, it never works. But that doesn't stop the child-abused adult. Sex and love become confused and often send a woman on a quest to find love using the only way she knows. In this I was very fortunate in that it was not my fate.

Had I succumbed, my life would have turned-out quite differently. The only thing that kept me from entering that darker world was being terrified of losing my mother's love. It was everything to me and I worked hard at being 'mummy's little helper'.

I did try to tell—in discreet ways. My art work for a start. Phallic symbols decorated my paintings or became abstract pottery masterpieces. As for my doodles—they were plain obscene! I couldn't be like the other girls, nor did I want to. I didn't want to look female. In fact I went through a phase of wanting a sex-change! It looked more fun being a boy—and maybe then I'd get noticed. Maybe then I'd matter.

Childhood also left me with the legacy that I should 'put others before myself'. This was reinforced by a Catholic upbringing in a Catholic school run by nuns. The legacy hangs around today. The difference is that, nowadays, I prioritise. Sometimes it's me, sometimes it's others. It's more of an informed choice. However, I know I prefer people to feel comfortable around me than not to. Maybe that's just human nature. I acquiesce less now I've discovered it's not rude or selfish to disagree.

It puzzles me that no-one wondered why a young girl like me didn't have a social life and just wanted to hang round her mum all the time. By now I was 15, gawky, skinny, tall and oh so shy. My dad nicknamed me 'Beanpole'. When my parents had people to dinner, my brother would entertain them all with fascinating stories of his ambitions. I'd just sit there, tongue-tied, long hair covering my face and with real butterflies in my stomach. My mother would say, afterwards, 'Why didn't you open your mouth and speak? Haven't you got a tongue in your head? You just sit there—in your shell. Everyone wants to know what you're doing with your life.' I wondered about that too. I'd feel deflated. My mum was beginning to get frustrated with me—that I wasn't turning into the girl she thought she was growing.

Shouting at a tortoise to come out of its shell will not get the tortoise to come out. It will retract further into its safe place. So there I stayed in my shell—for years. I remember talking to an aunt, once, trying to relate a story about something of no importance when suddenly my confidence leapt-up and rushed out of the door taking my voice with it. My aunt stared at me in anticipation but I just mumbled something and chased after them. It was ghastly. Crushing. But if you believe you're boring then you will relate whatever you have to say in a boring monotone voice and consequently *it will be boring*. It becomes a self-fulfilling prophecy which confirms your nothingness.

Christopher was in the top stream—I was in the second down, but I didn't mind. It just meant I had less work to do. Though not interested in any physical activity I was drawn to the music room. Sister Frances, the music teacher, always insisted on saying the entire rosary before the lesson could begin. After allowing for several interruptions we would finish just in time for the bell—and the end of the lesson. What a waste of time. I taught myself the guitar in spite of Sister Frances' prayers. It was the sixties and there were many riffs to learn.

Sister Frances and her rosary beads were replaced by the dynamic Miss Peskett and her guitar. Seeing how eager I was and how inadequate my little guitar was, the generous Miss Peskett (Ange as I'm allowed to call her now) bought me a new one. Or rather she gave me the money to buy a new one. So off I went to Hammonds in Queen's Street and handed over the cheque for the £26 Miss Peskett had given me in return for a gorgeous second-hand burnished six-string Hoyer. She told me recently that she only meant for me to spend about £8 and that I'd almost wiped out her savings, but she didn't have the heart to tell me at the time. Mum did repay her in little instalments. The guitar was a life-saver and her gift navigated me away from the rocks and installed in me a healthy obsession—but she didn't know it then. Neither did I. I played my heart out at assemblies, concerts and competitions. No-one could stop me. I loved every minute of it.

Freedom of sorts came in 1969 when my grandfather died. After two false endings, he finally departed this earth. The phone call from the hospital came at the dead of night as such phone calls always do. He had suffered a massive stroke. Dad wanted to go to the hospital. Wherever he went, he usually insisted mum went with him. The thought terrified the life out of me. To be left in the house by myself albeit with siblings, after my grandfather had died, was something I could not countenance. Might he appear as a ghost and threaten me not to tell? That was the one thing he was frightened of.

The terror of being a sitting target for a ghost was real. Then, out of the blue, mum came up with a suggestion, unaware of my plight. 'You were Grampie's favourite, darling. Would you like to go with dad?' I jumped at the chance. No way was I going to hang around here waiting for a phantasmal visitation.

There was an awkward silence in the car. Dad was immersed in his own grief. And I just sat there not knowing what to say. I certainly wasn't grieving—I wasn't even in two minds as to which state I'd prefer my grandfather to be in: alive or dead. I just felt awkward. But I did feel guilty for not feeling sad!

At the hospital the nurse pointed to the curtained bed. I didn't want to go in but as dad opened the curtain I caught sight of an enormous lump under the bedclothes. I saw its face—dark in death and ominous as ever. I'd never seen a corpse before. I was glad I glimpsed the body—to make sure he was definitely dead. Yes, He was dead. Phew!

It's amazing how guilt and blame etch themselves on our blueprint and become our default setting even when we haven't been abused in childhood. Writing this the inner me is thinking, 'Will the reader think I'm making too much of all this?' Then I remember Jane the lady I describe in *Chapter 8* who joined my self-help group in 1987. She asked if she 'qualified' to join as *all* her father did to her was to get her to stand naked in the middle of the room whilst he masturbated. Yet she struggled with alcohol, eating disorders and self-harming. The so-called severity doesn't matter. It's about the overpowering of a child, using sex as the weapon to achieve it. And, frequently, using the child's own sexuality as that weapon. Often an abuser will try to get the child's body to respond to stimulation thus rendering the child 'complicit' in her own abuse. Of course, it is not the case but an offender wants the child to feel at least partly responsible. It also assures her silence.

I felt my victim status was tattooed on my forehead. Since the abuse ceased and to date there have been 15 threatening situations in my life. From being followed (twice with my children in tow), assaulted in a lift, exposed to and, most recently, a lone visiting male paramedic trying it on whilst I was coming out of an atrial fibrillation episode!

However, in each case I saved myself. Somehow experience showed me that I didn't have to freeze and accept it anymore. Or maybe it was the fact that a stranger didn't have the same power over me as a grandfather. He didn't control my environment or the people in it.

When a man, probably in his twenties, pulled-up at the bus stop in his blue mini supposedly asking for directions, I went over to his car. It would've been impolite not to. As I got closer I could see what he was doing—and he was very busy doing it. I ran like hell towards to the safety of Uxbridge bus terminus. He turned his car around and pursued me in earnest. Down an alley I dashed only to find it was a dead-end. This was it—he was going to find me and that would be the end. He prowled round and round the terminus, headlights blazing, searching for me. It was pure luck that he didn't see me. He gave up and drove off. After about 20 minutes I emerged and leapt on the next bus out. It was ten o'clock at night and there was nobody around. When I got home I told no-one.

Then there was the flasher. I'd been doing a spot of hedge-trimming in my (maternal) grandma's front garden. My little brother was standing on a chair down the side of the house pretending to help. A young, blond man walked past—I thought he was nice-looking. A few moments later he appeared at the gate holding a map. Then he took the map away and yes—darrah! There it was—his pathetic manhood. Calmly, I went inside, shut the front door, and dashed around the side to rescue my brother. By now the flasher had moved and was standing at the top of the alleyway. I walked slowly up to my brother, picked him up and walked backwards to the house. As soon as I was in I locked the backdoor. What happened next belongs to one of Brian Rix's Whitehall farces.

My grandmother was standing with her back to the French windows and was facing me. This meant I could see the back garden but she couldn't. I stammered to tell her what had just taken place. At that moment I saw the man run through the back garden and over the fence. I stood and pointed, totally lost for words. By the time my grandmother turned round to see what it was I was pointing at, he'd gone — disappeared without a trace.

'What's the matter with you, child? Stop imagining things!' And the whole episode was dismissed. My brother couldn't back me up either! I'd been so calm that I don't think he noticed a thing. But I had acted brilliantly — no panic or hysteria — I just coped, and with success. Strangely, I didn't want anyone to ask too many questions anyway, in case I gave away too much sexual knowledge in my reply. Then they would know what my grandfather had been up to. I continued to protect 'our little secret' even after the pig died.

Aspects of Sexual Abuse

For people who have never experienced sexual abuse, I think it is important to emphasise some aspects of it. Sexual abuse has unique characteristics. Whilst sharing some effects with other forms of abuse, e.g. physical abuse, emotional abuse (being deprived of love), psychological abuse and mental abuse (mind games) — sexual abuse contains all these elements plus the added element of using, e.g. in the case of a child, the child's own sexuality as the weapon — as I've mentioned before. This is because a child cannot be sexually abused without also being emotionally, psychologically, mentally and in most cases physically damaged too.

Pick Up the Pieces

CHAPTER 4

Silly Me!

The case of the man in the lift occurred almost totally because of the voices in my head. Most of us will have a negative nagging narrator or two in our heads. It's usually the voice of a parent or sibling or some such figure of authority we've heard from birth. My own family adopted a kind of ribbing, chiding, mocking, at times ridiculing discourse throughout my early life. A feeble attempt at rhetoric, it probably wouldn't have had such an impact if it hadn't been for the abuse and its legacy of low self-esteem.

'Oh for goodness sake don't be daft', 'Stop being so silly', 'Don't imagine things', 'Nobody's looking at you', 'Stop being so sensitive', 'You're paranoid', etc., etc. These are phrases and clichés that I have heard forever and have clung onto, to keep myself from getting 'too big for my boots'. They sought to play down and dismiss my feelings — and distort my perception of the world.

Up until I'd read *Feel the Fear and Do It Anyway* by Susan Jeffers,[1] I used these voices most of the time. They were scolding, sneering, cynical, mocking, nasty voices that bullied and goaded me along. They gnawed at my self-confidence, made me doubt every word I uttered and every decision I attempted to make. The self-inflicted put-downs were constant and I fought them in vain. It was a sort of verbal flagellation. These words controlled me. Jeffers calls it The Chatterbox. I call it The Bully. They had been my companions for too long.

I don't think any of the contributors to these melded voices deliberately set out to hurt and I'd like to think they'd be horrified by what I did with

---
1. Vermillion, Revised edn. 2007.

their words and phrases. But, because they were heard and recorded in childhood, they have become part of my blueprint: these negative words are set in my hard drive. They were usually the first things that used to pop into my head in most situations. They are indelible. It's the way our hard drive is recorded. Therapy is an opportunity to re-record a new disc to counteract and overpower the original recording.

Whilst growing-up we absorb messages from every source. Sometimes we misinterpret them because we're only little and have no experience in how to be selective and filter things said to us. And with parents always trying to make us accept their version of reality, children have little choice but to discount their own perception of things. I remember hearing a psychologist say that *everything* we say to children has the potential to affect them. That is a scary thought. It means for certain that, as parents, there will be something that we will get wrong. Guaranteed. But there is no such assurance that we might get something right! We just have to hope.

So going down in the lift to the Post-Office at 5 pm when I was working at Savage & Parsons I felt uncomfortable about the man waiting by the front door of the offices. I walked past him and out into the street. After parting with the envelopes and packages I walked back to find he was gone. Phew that's a relief.

'Typical you,' said the scolding voice in my head.

'Typical me,' I concurred.

'Fancy thinking he was following you!'

'Fancy thinking he was following me'.

I went inside, pressed for the lift; the door opened and there he was.

'First floor?' he asked.

The fact that he spoke so matter-of-factly and with a smile instantly batted away the shock I felt when I saw him. Struggling to fight my inner feelings of doubt I stepped into the lift. And the voices in my head were not screaming, 'Get the hell out—this isn't safe'. No. They were sneering, 'Stop imagining things. Why would he be following *you*, for goodness sake? Stop being daft. It'll be fine. You're not the first person to get into a lift with a stranger are you? People do it every day'.

I recognised these blended voices. They were my mother, brother, father, Sister Ursula (maths) even my grandmother. And they were all screaming at me.

'First floor, please,' I asked, with a frozen smile.

As the lift came to a halt, he calmly put his arm across the door as the hand of his other arm was already making its way up my leg. Everything became a blur. Time stood still and rushed—it sort of crashed into itself. I took a deep breath, pushed his arm up, yanked the door open and got the hell out of there. At some point I heard myself shout a loud, prolonged, '*No!*' as I legged it up the stairs to my office.

My boss asked if I was okay as I clearly looked shaken but I just said I'd run all the way up the stairs—which was not untrue. I couldn't tell him why. I'd already started to feel stupid—stupid for *letting* it happen. The voices told me so.

When we are little and totally dependent on others, it's obvious that we're going to believe everything they tell us. We have nothing to compare it to or with. Adults use this opportunity to mould us into being malleable, obedient and controllable. It makes sense. 'Give me the boy until seven, and I'll give you the man'[2] is how the saying goes, which indicates that this is what we do with children. We condition them, brainwash them into being what we want them to be. Nothing wholly wrong with this; though to me it sounds a little sinister. We all need to know how to be a responsible, contributing member of society. But I think we instil our own values before a child has the chance of developing her or his own, we overdo it to the detriment and safety of the very children we're trying to protect.

In bringing children up to be 'good' we, at best, dilute their ability to rely on their own feelings and at worst completely replace their reality with our own interpretation. And we start it right from the off. For example: Little Johnny falls over and hurts his knee. He comes crying to mum or dad. 'There, there, that's not so bad. It's only a little cut. What's all the fuss about?' In Johnny's world, it blooming well hurts. 'But mummy is telling me it isn't hurting that badly. Mummy must be right.

---

2. Usually and originally attributed to Aristotle.

That means I must be wrong.' I know this is a rather simplistic example but what I'm trying to say is that we don't validate a child's perspective. We just assume they're wrong or even that they're lying. For example I remember hobbling around Kew Gardens as a six-year-old with a fractured foot. No one believed my incessant moaning.

Probably the most disconcerting incident occurred when I was with my daughter Lucy. She would have been eight at the time. We were walking through Dunstable market heading for the leisure centre to book a badminton session and I noticed a man following close behind. We crossed the road, he was still there; we went into the building and to the cashier. He was right behind us but when his turn came to be served he didn't respond. Leaving the centre he was still close. I looked at my daughter and thought, 'No, I can't ignore this situation.' I said nothing to her. Back at the market, I told a trader. 'Excuse me—that man is following us.' And bless him he promptly jumped out from behind his stall and confronted the individual.

'Oi, this young lady says you're following her!'

Blushing from ear –to-ear Mr Stalker stuttered, 'I'm f-from Houghton R...Regis'. Then, as luck would have it, a policeman appeared from nowhere. What are the chances of that? He too asked the suspect what he thought he was doing following us. After a few exchanges 'the man from Houghton Regis' was sent on his way. The obliging bobby offered to walk us back to the car but as I hadn't taxed it in a while I declined. Again, though, I had taken control of the situation and determined a different outcome. Lucy just found the drama funny.

I now understand that having been abused as a child I had absorbed the message that these things just happened to *me*. That somehow it was all *my* fault and there was something about *me*. In a strange way you feel more in control when it's all your fault. Fault and blame are familiar friends. Comforters even. Once you accept that, the effect resonates through your life until you seek help, and even then there are likely to be residual effects. It's much harder to live with anything being the other person's fault. We certainly can't let others take responsibility for what *they've* done—and can get quite possessive about fault and blame. It's ours and ours alone. Responsibility—power.

If you live your life feeling as though you don't belong or matter—that you're a horrible person, and you're to blame for the abuse—if you grow-up believing things that go wrong in your life are all your fault and that you hate yourself, then the persona you project will mirror these beliefs. *I feel like rubbish, I look like rubbish, people treat me like rubbish—so I must be rubbish.* It becomes a self-fulfilling prophecy and confirms all the negatives you believe about yourself.

Having little or no self-worth or confidence even affected my posture and the way I went about my daily life. I remember catching sight of myself walking past a shop window. I thought it was Fagin coming towards me. Stooped, eyes to the ground and practically pasted against the wall. I didn't want to be noticed. It didn't help that all my mum's efforts to improve me only made things worse.

'Why don't you buy a dress for a change and look feminine? You look like a freak in that. Why don't you sit up straight? Don't hunch! Speak clearly for goodness sake. Don't mumble, child'.

Comments any mother might make, though I don't think we should ever take such an accusatory approach with a child. These only served to make me feel further inadequate. I couldn't live up to her expectations. I was a disappointment to her; an embarrassment. While all her peers' daughters were thinking about their careers, I wanted to work in Fantos—the equivalent to the 'pound shops' of today but not as upmarket.

Sister Andrea, my English teacher, had hoped I too would become a teacher. I hoped to become a cleaner. Neither of us won. Mum pushed me through college to learn shorthand-typing. She was right. It held me in great stead, not necessarily career-wise but it is a skill you can take with you into anything. She had been a brilliant medical secretary. Mum was made for it. I, on the other hand, was hopeless at it. Being a secretary meant interacting with other people, answering the telephone, having a ready wit and being able to cope under pressure. There are no diplomas for staring at a wall.

It did not help that during my college years I had no money. Over-indulging his children was not a weakness of dad's. Whilst daughters of my parents' friends swished about in wrap-around skirts and wedge heels, I scuttled about in loons and plimsolls, ducking and diving so no-one would notice me. And I was right—they didn't. Well, not the people who could have helped. But it wouldn't have improved things had I had money. Because it wasn't really about money. I still would've bought weird clothes. They made me feel comfortable—in my rightful place. Nice modern clothes would only serve to make me feel worse as I didn't deserve to be wearing them: I was bad. I would actually feel sorry for the clothes if I bought them. How mad is that? My (maternal) grandmother could see that I needed a few things so she knocked me up a couple of pairs of flares on her Singer. The first and second pair were fine. The third were made from curtain material: Crimplene and sewn wrong side up. Not even I felt okay in those.

My social life as a teenager was poor during my teenage years at a time when it should have been exciting. I was more content being at home with my mum. She also needed help with the younger two. With a non-existent social life meeting boys was an improbability so it was handy having an older brother to furnish me with the occasional beau. There was one in particular. Sporting wild dark locks and moody Gibraltarian looks, Pete became my *must have*—and soon. Pete had lost his mum when he was twelve; life had not been kind to him. Then, aged eighteen, he'd had a massive row with his dad and now needed a place to stay whilst he sorted himself out. Cue Christopher. Pete was a van driver where Christopher worked and he felt sorry for him. So Christopher brought him home to stay until he found somewhere to live. We all made Pete welcome—particularly me.

It was not long before a romance blossomed between us. Mum was not best pleased. She had imagined someone totally different for me, her eldest daughter. But for me Pete was kind, flattering, an attentive listener and good for my low confidence. He was also available. Pete recognised and validated my qualities as a person in a way I had never experienced before. At first our relationship was very cloak-and-dagger but, eventually, we came clean.

Mum, realising Pete and I would not be parted, and suspecting that a pregnancy might ensue, now pushed for a wedding. So we tied the knot—but not very tightly—because nine months later we were the proud parents of the most beautiful baby boy I had ever seen. No matter that I'd spent the hottest summer on record looking and feeling like a beached whale. Adam was worth every degree Celsius.

Two years, two months, two days, two hours and two minutes later we were joined by the gorgeous little Lucy. Our family was complete. I loved being their mother. I still do.

But the clouds were gathering. We were living in Luton now, quite a way from my family. Pete was working night shifts and I was struggling to cope. I was lonely with no means of getting around without a car and the finances weren't terribly healthy. Depression was tip-toeing in. Something wasn't right and I suspected what it might be. Pete, realising that I was not happy in Luton, decided that it was time we moved back to Hemel Hempstead. Good choice. I began to feel better but still there was something. Something wasn't right.

Meanwhile life trundled on. The children got more beautiful as blooming little buds do. And Pete was knocking himself out at work for us. With the kiddies at school and nursery he found me a job: cleaning Mrs Boyer's house in the so-called *posh* area of Hemel. Mum was not best pleased. I know she was disappointed that I hadn't made a success of being a secretary. Though I thoroughly enjoyed the course, I didn't have the personality to go with it. But I gave it a go.

Prior to marrying Pete I had joined Renault in London as a terrible secretary. And boy, was I bad. The phone terrified me, the boss terrified me and with my excessively wet, sweaty hands, the electric typewriter terrified me. The longer I stayed at Renault the more inept I became. So I palled-up with Sophie Millar, another secretary, and we would spend our days walking around other departments, chatting and drinking tea. Or we'd pootle over to Kensington High Street for a mooch. I am astonished we didn't get the sack. Happy days!

Now I was hoovering and dusting another woman's house. But I liked it. There was no responsibility. I certainly had the personality for this—having no ambition whatsoever. Pete was pleased that I was contributing financially at last. I had wanted to be a stay-at-home mum partly because I wanted to hide from the world. But there was no chance of that—we needed the money.

Although I was technically an adult, being firmly secured to our extended family made me feel like a big child. Important decisions were generally vetted by my parents before we made them. Pete was not comfortable with this but went along with it. I was far too weedy to have an opinion. I thought I had a choice, but looking back I see the choices I made were to fit in with everyone else. I had the illusion of autonomy. At the time it felt okay because I didn't want the responsibility of big decision-making anyway. Like a little limpet I would consult my mother on everything from what to make for dinner to where we should live. I allowed myself to be controlled.

Growing-up in our family was a bit like living in a goldfish bowl. I felt we had to portray a certain image to my parents' friends: a nice, perfect family. I didn't feel we were real: no sibling arguments and differences — it felt to me that we were almost pretending. There was no freedom to rebel within our family. We had to be frightfully proper. For me it felt artificial. Christopher and I were both painfully self-conscious — we still are.

Pete's family is a great example, however, of how familial disagreement and arguments can be a force for good. When he and his siblings were growing-up after their mother died they were pretty much left to fend for themselves. Inevitably there were fights and squabbles, but from that they learned how to be *real*. They forged unbreakable bonds which have held them in great stead. They are always there for each other. Today there is a genuine affection and respect for one another which I can only envy.

Mum, having been the powerful matriarch in her own family since the death of her father, had learned how to govern with a capital G. And no-one would question her authority on anything. Why would they? Her decisions were always the right ones. Getting me to learn shorthand-typing was one example. They're excellent skills which I use today. *Your mum is always right* is not a cliché but a fact.

Time rolled on and once Lucy was at nursery I joined the Halifax as a secretary. Yes, I'd listened to mum again and was back in an office doing my worst. I was struggling with my colleagues being nice and wanting to include me. *If they knew what I was really like* followed me everywhere. My coping strategies were, like the walls of the House of Usher, beginning to crumble. I was empty inside and exhausted with keeping up the façade. But there was nothing behind this façade, this mask. The anger in me was beginning to well-up, dangerously so.

I was twenty-seven when I disclosed what had happened to me as a child. I had sensed myself withdrawing from the extended family life for a while now. I realise that what I was experiencing was a healthy pull away from the old administration that had suffocated me since forever. I was beginning to resist and reject all that had been foisted upon me without my consent. There is no doubt I had been controlled by my family. My life up until now was all about being a good daughter, sister, granddaughter, niece, laundress—having to conform to impossible demands whilst ignoring the carelessness which resulted in my being abused. My joy was my children but I felt they deserved better than this mother they'd ended-up with. Then, one evening, after the children had gone to bed and Pete was out walking the dog, I opened my diary and wrote, in yellow felt pen, 'Bastard'. I closed the book and put it back on the shelf. 'Ha!' I thought, 'nobody can stop me writing that. And I could always close the book to protect the secret. His secret. But soon it wasn't enough. Questions began to swirl around unanswered in my head. Why me? What had I done? Why didn't I tell? I must have been invisible as a child—no, not invisible—*unimportant.*

Then Coral, my sister, came to stay. I loved her company—she was easy to be with and excellent with the children. After we'd dropped them at school one morning we'd come home and were enjoying a cup of coffee. Suddenly, and unexpectedly for both of us, I told her I'd been abused from the age of seven. I just opened my mouth and the words galloped out. I didn't have to do a thing. Her jaw dropped and she looked horrified. Horrified not at me but that it had happened to me.

'Who?' she asked. I told her. She was shocked. Coral remained calm and serene. It was so assuring. She didn't bolt or question anything I'd said, it was all about me. She listened, smiled, nodded. She believed me. Wow! She believed me. What a moment in history. The road to being healed had begun. And it felt strange indeed.

A few evenings later she was watching a programme with my mum about abuse. When it was over she turned off the telly and quietly told mum that there was someone in our family who that had happened to.

Mum's reaction was astonishing. Shockingly, she 'guessed' that it was I who had been the victim; and secondly she identified the abuser as my *grandfather*.

When Coral told me this I didn't know what to think or feel. Anger, hurt, shock, horror, betrayal, disappointment — a storm of emotions and questions bombarded me. Mum had known all along? She didn't protect me, ask me, comfort me, she didn't tell anyone — what on earth was going on? Was I not worth protecting? Was I really so insignificant? I'd always felt insignificant — now there was proof.

It took a long time to process it all. Mum and I spoke. She said she only *thought* that something might have happened. She wasn't sure. At the time she'd noticed my behaviour change from a spirited little girl to a withdrawn, quiet little mouse. Yet, still she didn't do anything. She didn't investigate or question anything — probably hoping it would all go away if she ignored it. Who would believe her? He was her husband's father after all: her father-in-law. And what could be done anyway? How would she tell Joe what she thought his father might be up to? No real evidence, only uncomfortable feelings. I asked myself time-and-time-again — how could she *not* do or say anything?

The answer only became clear much later after I joined a survivors' self-help group. It was in Essex. By now I had told Pete about the abuse and he was so supportive and kind to me. He would drive me all the way to Essex for my sessions, waiting patiently outside. And I can still remember with clarity the overwhelming feeling of belonging when I sat with these other women. For the very first time in my life I felt comfortable... and I was able to 'open my mouth and speak'. And to a *group* of people too. They listened; they smiled; they nodded; they ummed and ahhd and it was so, so wonderful. I couldn't believe what I was feeling. The rapport was tangible. Is this what it feels like to be normal? I was suddenly no longer tongue-tied; I opened my mouth and words came out! I had found my tongue — it had been hiding in my head all the time! I will be forever grateful to those ladies. My confidence quickly grew. And grew.

Although my mother was initially quite supportive she began to try and influence my progress. I was three months into the counselling and moving away from her control. She felt uncomfortable. I understood. The status quo was changing. My mother thought the counselling was going to give her back a nice malleable daughter. She couldn't cope with this renegade. My first counsellor observed that my mother was over-involved in my life. I think she rightly deduced this when I brought her along for my second counselling session.

I can't remember if she ever gave me an explanation as to how and why she didn't do anything at the time of the abuse, but an answer of sorts came from the group I attended. It was to do with her being a victim too, in a sense. What would have happened if she'd told my father? He was the only breadwinner at the time. Who'd believe her? Where was the evidence — only a seven-year-old's word against the head of the family. He would deny it and then where would she be? And hadn't Charmaine been known to lie? Didn't she once steal a pig from the nursery farmyard? Didn't she nick flowers from nextdoor's garden? Put like that it began to make sense. But my mother was an adult — if she found it hard to tell, how on earth was I, a seven-year-old, powerless little girl expected to tell. There was far too much at stake — and anyway what words would I use?

It was tough accepting this but, logically, they were right. However, it got me thinking about how we condition children and turn them into sitting targets for abusers. Surely, there must be something we could do? This was an unspoken area: the way we bring up children and its impact on abuse which I return to in later chapters.

My father was eventually told about what had happened in my childhood. He'd begun to be curious concerning what was going on — the phone calls and whispering, etc. — he hated being kept out of the loop. One day when he was in the garden weeding mum went out and told him, just like that. Apparently he threw down his gloves and stormed inside.

'Who?' Who did this to *his* daughter?

'Your father,' mum told him.

Now I might have been naïve or too optimistic, but the response I thought it would evoke would have been something along the lines of 'My poor child, how could this have happened to my little girl, what a bastard to have done that to his own granddaughter!' I was wrong.

Instead, his reaction centred on himself. It was, 'How could my father do this to *me*? How could he have betrayed *me* like this?'

Where was *I* in all this? And most astonishingly of all he revealed, 'I knew he couldn't be trusted but I thought he would have respected *me* at least.' Wow, this was another bombshell. Dad suspected his own father couldn't be trusted, based on what I don't know. But I believe he thought that because he was a *revered* son his own daughter would be out of bounds—that's if he saw it that way. It was a case of I'll show my dad how much I love and respect him by trusting him with my daughter—by giving her to him. Anyway, he asked to see me. Here comes the, 'My darling daughter, I'm so sorry', bit I thought with mixed anticipation.

When I arrived he gave me a hug. Any sort of hug from him was unusual so I thought we were off to a good start. This greeting, however, promised something different altogether. We walked down to the pub, which I thought was an odd thing to do for a start. He had a whisky then opened the conversation—in a misguided *defence* of his father.

'He was old, didn't know what he was doing, he probably didn't mean to.' I was flabbergasted. And he rounded it off with, 'Does this mean that, if I had nowhere to live, you wouldn't give me a home?'

I struggled at first to understand what he meant. Then it dawned on me. Basically, he was asking me that because of what his father did would I now trust *him* with my children by letting him live with us if he was homeless. I was speechless. But instead of answering like I might have done before by appeasing him with, 'Oh daddy of course I trust you and of course I'd have you live with us,' I bravely shook my head incredulous at the suggestion and let the silence speak for itself. The fact is I would trust dad but I could never let him know that.

If my dad couldn't come up with a reason for his father's abusive behaviour then my later study of sex-offenders did. My grandfather had targeted me because I was unprotected and vulnerable. He must've seen something about me and/or how distant my relationship with my father was; he knew how well-respected and loved he was and enjoyed life on his pedestal. How confident must he have been that he could get away with it given that he was broke, homeless and old with a dodgy heart? Yet he still felt sure he could get away with it without being caught. Had my grandfather seen a close bond between father and daughter I don't see how he would have risked it. Why would he? And how did he know I wouldn't tell?

Without a doubt he had it all worked out and I find that chilling. It would have all been orchestrated with him controlling every person in the family. More than likely it would have been a behaviour well-practiced — a path frequently trodden. My grandfather had done his homework so he could walk with confidence. He saw I was alone and he further isolated me from my family by giving me what I craved — paternal affection and attention. He put on a brilliant performance of the poor old pensioner, loving father and doting grandfather. He portrayed himself as a victim. He won my mother's respect and pretty much managed everybody in the family. Shocking. Shocking that he could do it in the first place and shocking that he could get away with it.

My parents couldn't take in what had happened to their daughter or accept that they might have protected me better. I don't think many parents in such a situation do. That is not a criticism — it's too painful for them and they couldn't live with the guilt. I, on the other hand, had grown-up with guilt — it has been my loyal companion these 60 years. Enlightening my parents was not worth pursuing. I'd rather put my energies into me. My parents are not exonerated for their part in the abuse. It was a carelessness that resulted in a life-changing experience for me.

In 1995 a journalist contacted my parents about a book she was writing about my grandfather. Apparently, he'd discovered a precious stone which was now on display in the Science Museum in London. She wanted to interview my parents and they were happy to be involved. They'd even asked my son Adam if he'd mind doing some research for them. Adam declined. I found their eagerness to be involved puzzling to say the least.

My confidence blossomed with the help of the Essex group and now with the Hemel group thriving and expanding I was beginning to know what success felt like. The local press was behind us and would occasionally run stories and invite us to comment on related issues. Although under the wing of the National Society for the Prevention of Cruelty to Children (NSPCC), we were pretty much free to develop as we wanted.

Once a month I would meet up with a social worker for a catch-up and that's why I was at the NSPCC offices that fateful morning.

The waiting room in the NSPCC was suddenly quiet — the whirlwind had left the building. I pondered Mr Wyre's request for a 'survivor' to appear with him on telly. Me, on the telly? No I couldn't do it. I'd talk to the girls at the (survivor's) group, maybe one of them would. I wasn't ready for my TV debut. But who was this Ray Wyre, this tornado on legs?

CHAPTER 5

'Hello Sailor'

Raymond Keith Wyre was born in a nursing home in Bournemouth on 2nd November 1951, the younger of two sons. His father Derek was a Chief Petty Officer, his mum Ada a housewife. On his first day at school an apprehensive little Ray had hung-up his coat next to the other children's and then came running back to his mum, arms open wide, for one last hug, saying in an tear-choked voice, 'Nother love, mummy?'

His description of his childhood was that it was a bit Huckleberry Finn-ish with lots of freedom and adventures. Saturday mornings were spent at the cinema with armfuls of sweeties and coke. One Christmas, for a present, his parents said they would get his old bike repaired. Not disappointed with this, he looked forward to seeing his old bike in working order come the day. Instead, on descending downstairs on Christmas morning, little Ray found a brand new blue bicycle waiting for him under the tree. He was thrilled.

In 1967, after living in Belfast for a few years due to his dad's posting, Ray followed his father into the Royal Navy and became a sea-cadet. By the time he was 15 he was out on the ocean waves as Junior Control Electrical Mechanic (2nd Class) Wyre. He was a mere rating which, in his own words, was 'on par with a bilge rat'. Those who know him will accept that Ray was a bit calamitous. Accidents just 'happened' to him. So it was brave of the Navy to make him an electrician. It was a potentially lethal combination: electricity, water and Ray.

His turn to cook breakfast on board ship went awry when he mistook washing powder for porridge. And as he was cooking-up for the whole crew, he'd put numerous large scoops in the pot and waited for the expected breakfast to develop. Instead an ensuing frothy mess bubbled and bubbled endlessly, oozing over the pot onto the floor heading for the door. It was like *The Magic Porridge Pot*. Apart from a few unfortunate accidents, Ray and the Navy survived his time there with him leaving with only a tattoo.

From 1968 to 1970, he served on *HMS London*. Life on the ocean waves introduced him to a seedier side of life that he could never have imagined. He was shocked and appalled by the depravity he came across in the naval ports.

In 1970, Ray returned briefly to Belfast but it no longer felt like home because of The Troubles which had begun again in previous year. So he signed up for the submarines—*HMS Valiant* as Control Electrician Mechanic (1st Class). Years later we visited a submarine in dock and I plucked up the courage to go inside. It was claustrophobic. Amongst all the nautical paraphernalia there sat two torpedoes poised and ready for action. And there didn't seem to be enough bunks for 60 sailors. There weren't. Ray explained that they had to 'hot-bed': when one rating was on duty another would sleep in his bed. Yuk. Too much information. It baffles me how all those men could live in such a confined space with no daylight, fresh air or proper washing facilities. One can only imagine the fug bursting out when the lid was lifted.

It was while he was ashore in Plymouth in Aggie Weston's, the pastoral charity for seamen, that Ray found his Christian faith. Being medically discharged because of injuries to his feet, he enrolled at Birmingham Bible College. At the end of his course he could be officially ordained—but, again, fate played a hand. During this three years Ray had been doing some work as a probation volunteer; he'd also become disillusioned with organized religion. Then, after being inspired by a talk given by someone from the Probation Service, he began studying for his Certificate in Social Work.

By now he was married with a family and needing to earn a better living. Soon he was working at Albany Prison on the Isle of Wight. It was while he was seeing prisoners on probation that he realised the information they were sharing in the waiting-room about their sexual offending was something that was being lost: information on how offenders target and groom their victims—how they control their environment in order to abuse. Ray recognised that this information needed to be collected and channelled so he began a therapy group for these men to address their behaviour. From 1981, he specialised in working with sex-offenders. It was his interest in these clients that eventually led him to leave the Probation Service and not very quietly. None of the probation hierarchy wanted him to work with sex-offenders. From there he joined a stellar group of professionals to create the Gracewell Clinic.

I'm not sure what he was doing at the NSPCC that day when we met in the waiting-room but it was a fortuitous meeting. The girls at the Hemel group agreed to a meeting about appearing on the programme Ray had mentioned. After much discussion, however, we declined the offer to take part. In hindsight I think we were being a bit too precious and missed a great opportunity to put our views forward.

Some of us in the group were taking counselling courses and improving the service we were offering. We also decided to hold a talk-night every month which meant inviting someone related to the work to come and speak to us. One month it was a police officer, another month it was a counsellor from Luton Rape Crisis and another month it was Ray Wyre. Needless to say Ray's talk went down a storm. Nobody wanted to leave at the end of the evening.

The Role of the Dice

It is interesting that the two most influential men in my life, i.e. Ray and my grandfather were both prolific gamblers. My grandfather was a casino addict. He lost his entire gem collection, and even the precious stone he'd discovered, to the dice. Though he was an intelligent man he clearly enjoyed taking risks—as his sexual abuse of me demonstrates. For him to take the risk of sexually abusing me paid off. He was not caught out in his lifetime and thus got away with it.

Ray, too, was a dedicated gambler and justified this by claiming that as he didn't drink, smoke or have any other hobbies, what he spent at casinos amounted to how much he would have spent on a hobby. Most gamblers find a way of defending their habit. However, as his bank accounts later showed, he too lost far more than he ever won. After all, no casino would give him a suite of rooms for 'free' if they weren't certain of getting their money back. Of this courtesy, Ray was proud—he even videoed the rooms to show me on his return!

So, the *role* of the dice has played a significant part in my life even though I have never succumbed myself.

I have often been asked whether there is a link between my relationship with Ray and my relationship with my grandfather. Both were risk-takers. And both were involved in the world of sexual abuse. Having given this much thought, I believe that there may be a tenuous connection in that the latter sexually abused and the former rescued the abused. Subconsciously I might have been hoping to recreate a situation from my past but one, this time, over which I could have control and power and succeed—I could create a different outcome. However, looking back I don't think there are any winners. The risk-taking for both paid off for them in one way or another. My grandfather got away with abusing and Ray got away from the colossal financial debts he left behind him. Seen like that it would appear that both 'threw a six'.

CHAPTER 6

Moving On

The busier I became in my new life the more distant Pete and I grew. After leaving the factory he'd been with for ten years he became a chauffeur for the boss. He loved doing this work, but now the boss had retired. Pete was made redundant so he set up his own taxi business with his redundancy money. His time and enthusiasm were entirely focused on Beacon Cars. I knew that once he was absorbed in his world and mixing with people things between us would change. In saying this, I know I'm implicating him in the demise of our marriage. I hope so, because carrying the entire burden of responsibility for the end of us is just too onerous. Even if I'd remained at the Halifax and Pete hadn't been made redundant I still couldn't see us lasting. I wished I could have loved him in the way he wanted. But I had tried.

Meanwhile, a vacancy came up at the Luton Rape Crisis Centre mentioned earlier and Jan, the co-ordinator, asked if I'd like to join them. I accepted. My days there were without doubt the happiest of my working life. The empowerment they gave me and anyone who went there was inspirational. It was a wonderful atmosphere. Refreshing. The door was always open. I loved the flow and mix of people — I grew and learned so much about myself and life in general. It was intoxicating.

The centre gave me a free hand to do whatever I wanted to. So, I started a group for family members of someone who discloses abuse. This led to the making of *The Other Victim* — a video focusing on their dilemma. The general media was interested in it and the video received a lot of publicity and positive feedback. There were articles about it in *Cosmopolitan* and *Community Care*, etc. and even a TV appearance. Then there were the conferences and workshops which I organized and spoke at. From

Bramshill Police Training College (as it was then) to A&E departments, social services to family centres, I would talk about the effects of sexual abuse to anyone who'd listen. We were even privileged to be asked to give talks in schools. This was important work. Empowering children and giving them an awareness was something deeply important to me and still is.

Lister Hospital and Letchworth Mental Health Unit employed me as their sexual-abuse counsellor. From another conference I was invited to join Asplands Medical Health Centre in Woburn Sands also as their sexual abuse counsellor. And somewhere along the way I did my diploma in counselling. With my workload increasing I decided to leave the Luton centre altogether and work independently.

As always with work like this, there are often some clients whose stories stay with you forever. 'Alice' was one. She was diagnosed with psychosis and wouldn't respond to her male clinical psychologist. He had the insight to realise this match was not going to work because she didn't trust men, so he referred her to me. For the first three sessions she would just sit on the edge of the chair, her hair covering her face, and staring down into space. After many almost silent sessions she began to sit further back in the chair—her voice still feint. Bit by bit she started to ease up. The progress was so slow it was hardly noticeable. In time she began to release her story—and it had, unsurprisingly, been horrific.

Alice had been raped at the age of 14 by two 'friends' and, because of her upbringing, submerged the ordeal into her very core. She self-harmed believing that the rape was her fault—and was still doing this. My respect for her was immense—that she'd had the courage to start talking about it now. I listened with all my heart. What struck me about Alice was how she had been moulded into this victim by her parents well before the rape had taken place. Her upbringing/conditioning had compounded the damage she experienced in the rape.

As an only child of older doctor parents, Alice was left almost totally to the transient care of a string of nannies. She felt unloved, unheard, unseen for most of her early life. Yet she tried desperately to be accepted and acceptable to her parents. It was tragic. Her rigid upbringing included being beaten, never being believed, being left in the dark to cry—the list was endless. Nevertheless, she kept justifying her parents' behaviour, minimising it and trying to make everything her fault. She got pregnant at 17 and was thrown-out. Homeless and penniless with a baby on the way, Alice had to fend for herself. It chokes me up now to think of it.

In the sessions, Alice found a space where she could be Alice. She could talk and be heard, hold eye-contact and even, eventually, laugh. Three years on and dear Alice was sitting back in her chair, hair brushed away from her face, looking at me, talking aloud and occupying the whole room. And I discovered she had a wicked sense of humour. She owned her space. I felt so privileged to have accompanied her on her journey for those three years. She still needed that space where once a week she could be Alice for an hour — but the service was cut and the sessions terminated. I know that she went on to get a job after being unemployed for several years but I'm gutted at the abrupt ending of the sessions. I hope she found another 'Alice space' in which to thrive. She had a lovely gentle energy and so much to give.

There are many more Alices I could talk about but the one thread that links all of them together is their upbringing and conditioning: their total lack of tools and confidence with which to face the world. Alice found it hard to see her parents' neglect as having an impact on the rape and how she dealt with it — or the knock-on effects caused by their treatment of her. Her case, as with others, highlights the need for a review of how we condition children and the language we use in that conditioning. I still have the beautiful paperweight she gave me at our last session. I will always treasure it.

People have often asked me how I could listen to tragic stories without being affected. The analogy of someone splashing about, drowning in the rapids is a good one that demonstrates the role of a counsellor. The drowning person will not be rescued by someone else jumping into the rapids to save them. They will both drown. No, the role of a counsellor is to secure herself to a tree using a strong winch, then to reach down into the rapids to help her client. Only by remaining safe and secure can a counsellor be of any effective purpose.

Also, how a listener reacts when someone discloses abuse is hugely important. A vacant look can convey an opinion that the abuse isn't horrific. A client told me that when she disclosed to a friend she got what she believed was a cool (minimising) response. This confirmed to my client that the abuse she'd endured wasn't all that bad and that she'd been over-reacting. However, a highly-charged emotional reaction can make the discloser feel robbed of expressing that level of emotion for themselves: after all she will have been the one experiencing it.

What each discloser wants is a response that reflects the seriousness of what is being disclosed because the discloser hasn't, up until now, been able to evaluate the seriousness of her/his abuse for themselves. They are in need of an outside view to put it into some kind of perspective. So the listener has quite a task. In an instant the listener has to convey shock, horror, understanding, sympathy and empathy whilst remaining calm and grounded — and make sure the 'horror' reaction is interpreted as horror towards the abuse not the abused. It's quite tricky. Honesty is probably a safe option.

The talks I gave to schools are something I'm glad I did. Not being a natural orator, they frightened the hell out of me but what emerged was the difference in the questions between the boys and the girls. At the age of 14 the boys were already asking that, if a woman was wearing a short skirt and walking home alone late at night drunk, wasn't she partly responsible if she was attacked. The girls in the group tended not to ask too many questions at all but hung around afterwards to chat. Again, the issue of language kept presenting itself. These youngsters had already been hugely influenced by inaccurate language which had moulded them into people who believed the stereotypical roles set out for them. The boys tended to be full of bravado and questioning whether rape was wholly the fault of the man; the girls seemed comfortable with accepting some of the responsibility for rape. And neither gender knew sufficiently how to 'trust their own feelings' or to recognise them when they felt uncomfortable in a situation.

The feedback forms evinced where future work needed to be done but, once again, funding was cut and the all too important talks didn't continue.

CHAPTER 7

Ray and Me

Ray's new single status in the mid-1990s and my crumbling marriage meant that we were on a collision course towards each other — like two love-struck dreadnoughts. It's no secret that I became besotted with him. This infatuation was born out of my immense respect for his work. Whether this was healthy or not remains to be seen — but we had to be in each other's lives. If he'd ask me to walk on hot coals, I would have done that — and without shoes. My feelings towards him were all-consuming.

Ray, with his knowledge of abuse and abusers, represented the issue of my own abuse. He was not a sex-abuser, that is not what I'm saying, but he *represented* the issue of my abuse. Therefore, being with him was, in a complex way, about me confronting and overcoming my abuse but with a different ending. It was no easy ride, for sure, even though we loved each other. We moved in together in 1997 and married in 1999.

I cannot fully understand my excessive attraction towards him (I am not alone in this conundrum) other than his fatal charisma. He was a bit of a Marmite, really — you either loved him or you didn't. I, unfortunately, loved him to destruction. But this was a reciprocal love that was hugely detrimental to both of us. Truly, madly, deeply doesn't touch it. For my part I wanted to own him, possess him — overpower him even. I didn't want him to leave my side. He was equally possessive but was more subtle about it.

Ray flooded me with affection, charm and indulgence — decadent indulgence. During our first food-shop together he said, 'Get whatever you want'. I burst into tears in the middle of Sainsbury's. Never in my life had I heard those words before. What a novelty — to not have to buy the cheapest burgers, margarine, lard. But that was Ray all over. To have what you want is how he lived his life — and to have it now. He flooded our relationship with excess and this appealed to my selfish side.

And he just oozed fun. He could always see the funny side of everything. Humour was one thing we definitely shared. Ray did harbour a concern, however, that I might abandon him. I think he believed that no-one could sustain this intensity of emotions I demonstrated towards him. So, in a way the 'having what you want' might also have been about securing me and as such could feel controlling. Only when I tried to do things independently of him did I realise there was indeed a control issue. But that has only been a recent discovery. No matter. At the time I revelled in his affection and attention. I became painfully possessive. Even his colleagues and friends commented that they didn't see so much of him anymore — that he had become inaccessible to them.

Being curled up in front of the telly together was bliss for us. But there was one major intrusion: his work. Ray's work was not just his life, but also his wife. She could accompany him anywhere, she was always welcome. People were interested in her. She never let him down or spoke out of turn. And she was happy to stay up until the small hours with him and his audience. He was proud of her and could control the situation completely. They were the perfect match — inseparable.

I, on the other hand, had little to contribute in comparison. After all what could I say that was at least equal to what Ray Wyre had to say. On social occasions I would feel like a waitress in my own home. Guests would be enthralled by him. When I shared my feelings of shyness with Ray he was surprised. His suggestion was that I should just cut across the conversation and throw in my penny's worth. The thought was as ridiculous as it was terrifying. Imagine the scene: he's holding forth to our dinner guests about the complex psychology of some psychopathic murdering rapist and I would interrupt with, 'Would you like to see my vintage Citroen Dyane? It's only ever had one previous owner.' It just wouldn't work.

I thought we could read *You Just Don't Understand* by Deborah Tannen[1] in order to help us (i.e. him) understand the issue of misunderstanding

---

1. Virago Press Ltd, 1991.

between men and women (i.e. us) in conversation. Good idea I thought. It would bring us closer together, I thought. We each had a copy. By page 34 we were in disagreement; by page 40 we were arguing; by page 45 we'd given up. Or rather he had given up and I was too nervous to pursue it further. But I did get something out of it. The book showed me just how differently men and women communicate. Men tend to 'report' talk and women tend to 'rapport' talk. With that basic understanding under my belt, I coped much better in my conversations with men. I don't allow myself to feel quite so intimidated.

Christmas was a divine event with no expense spared. Not only did he give the biggest presents but he also expected to receive the biggest presents and buying for him became a nightmare. There was no such thing as too big — or too expensive. I think that by buying everyone what they wanted, Ray was actually giving to himself. He was incredibly childlike. One year my daughter bought him a fibre optic table lamp. When I came up to bed that night I found the room in darkness bar the lamp. Lying curled in the foetal position and staring-up enchanted by the changing, sparkly colours Ray was absorbed — with the sweetest expression of a child. That this colossus of a man who could bring down any conniving, murderous rapist could also be this innocent child delighting in the pretty lights was beautiful to see. The contrast epitomises what he was all about — this child/man, Ray Wyre — my husband. That image will always stay with me.

Ray was becoming a world-renowned expert by now and had recently begun making regular lecture tours to Australia. These lasted six weeks at a time and obviously the hosts didn't want to pay for his wife to accompany him — so I stayed home. Six weeks without my life-support system was incredibly traumatic for me. I'd be counting the days, hours until I set eyes on him again. And when he finally walked through Arrivals at Heathrow I would unashamedly burst into tears of relief. Was this love or obsessive dependency? Who's to know? But my feelings towards Ray controlled my life and I was degenerating into an emotional wreck.

During our marriage, my personal journey was not only on-hold, but had actually regressed. I stopped achieving and being creative. His desire to be involved in every idea I had made me feel undermined and inadequate. As though he didn't have confidence in my ability even though, prior to us getting together, I had achieved a great deal on my own in terms of personal and professional growth. Now there was a power struggle going on between us and I was beginning to feel under his control as I had done with my parents.

Discussions with Ray could be scary. It felt like he could argue his point to within an inch of my life. And even when I conceded defeat it wouldn't mean the discussion was over. There was no place in our marriage where we could talk about our power struggle. I wouldn't like to believe that Ray deliberately set out to control me. I think being in control was something he sought in every situation whilst giving the illusion that he was not. The ability to do this stemmed, I'm sure, from his own insecurity which is why he needed his work-wife beside him at all times. She was comforting and reassuring. With her next to him he felt powerful, useful, successful. At family gatherings, shopping, dining-out, even at the cinema, Ray and work-wife always stole the show. I would have felt jealous, had I had the confidence.

The only area I excelled in was cooking and looking after his daily personal needs. Picking-up discarded needles from his diabetic testing-kit always annoyed me. And it was dangerous. The dogs could easily have trodden on them. So, I factored disposing needles into my daily routine amongst other things a wife shouldn't really have to do. I had become a mere appendage again and felt I was disappearing in his shadow.

Standing next to a mountain you stand in a shadow. There is no sunlight to warm you, feed your energy, lift your spirits or allow you to grow; you shrink and your spirit depletes. Eventually you begin to wilt. That's how I felt towards the end of living with Ray. I had to act to save myself before it was too late. So we lived separately for a short while. There was no-one else for either of us and we were always going to remain husband and wife. I knew I couldn't exist without him in my life no matter how hard I tried. My fast-dissipating confidence became painfully obvious during a conference he'd put on in 2001.

There he was being Ray Wyre whilst I couldn't speak to anyone—I couldn't mingle, there was nothing left inside me. I was tongue-tied. No confidence, nothing to say. The subject was obviously familiar to me but whereas, not so long ago, I would have chatted and laughed with the delegates and got involved—now I was thrown back in time to silence. I recognised this place. And I didn't want to be there again. It felt as though I had failed. Well, at least as a failure I had succeeded.

In his colossal shadow, I felt but a minnow. When I accompanied him to conferences and meetings I was insignificant. Invisible. Nobody wanted to talk to me. In fact I was an encumbrance—a bit of a spare part. At one conference the organizer suggested I go shopping instead of 'hanging around'. This did wonders for my self-esteem. They just wanted Ray to themselves. I could certainly identify with that. It's all I wanted too. I just wanted us to be at home on the sofa massaging each other's feet and watching *Goodnight Sweetheart* on a loop.

Tumbling into the abyss again, the self-harming returned. Nothing major but digging my nails into the palm of my hand or my neck became an outlet for the anger I felt towards myself. I blamed myself for not being confident and capable anymore. I was disappointed in me. In my childhood I had done the same but it was not nearly as severe. Now I left marks. I wanted to see evidence that I'd been duly punished. I was also becoming aware that Ray's friends, family and colleagues saw me as a bit of an appendage, a nuisance—that I had taken him away from them. To a certain extent this was true. I had wanted him all to myself and didn't realise that Ray was really married to the world—not just me. Unlike Princess Diana who only had three people in her marriage, I had thousands.

In the first year of our marriage I developed Crohn's disease. During one flare-up I was admitted to hospital. Because these incidents were becoming so frequent, Ray suggested that I give up the counselling and lead a sedentary life. He painted an idyllic picture of dogs, country walks, fields, a camper van—all very tempting. 'Give it up, darling. I'll look after you,' were his exact words. Who could refuse?

I gave up the counselling contracts I had earned on my own merit and declined the offer of sole counsellor for Mid-Bedfordshire Eating Disorder Clinic which had just been offered to me. Everything I had achieved independently was gone. In their place were telephone staff support contracts with various organizations—all procured by Ray. But these were not used to capacity. They were in place 'just in case' staff needed them. They were assurances against staff litigation. But I struggled with the feeling that as they were not used to capacity I was not giving value for money. This impacted on my already diminishing confidence and challenged my integrity.

Only now do I see the abuser/victim scenario that was being re-enacted in our relationship. There was a power struggle going on and one of us was going to lose. My odds were on it being me. By my choosing to separate from him eventually, I rescued myself. As a romance we were second to none—wonderfully sweet and beautiful. As an equal partnership it was fraught—but as a marriage it was disastrously doomed. However, we could not exist purely as a romance—it would not survive as life got in the way. Practical day-to-day living with Ray became an insurmountable hurdle.

And why was he so good at extracting the truth from psychopaths and rapists? Was it really a natural gift or something more sinister? To date no-one has come close to his expertise. There are lots of excellent programmes being developed by brilliant therapists. But there is no Ray Wyre. There is no chain-clanking in the face of bigotry and dangerous narrow-mindedness. Just an ominous silence.

Journalist Sally Vincent's description of him is the best and most accurate I have ever read. She wrote an article in the *Observer* (or it may have been the *Guardian*) circa 1990 entitled 'The House of Loathing' in which she perfectly encapsulated his brilliance. She noted of his Gracewell business partnership that Trevor Price, his collaborator and the business brains behind Gracewell, was sharp, dapper and yuppyish whilst Wyre was podgy, with finger-marks on his spectacles and his shirt hanging out, 'two halves of a genius!' After observing Ray interviewing a sex-offender, she described him as 'The matador performing a psychic excavation that would take the ordinary therapist three years to do what [he] does in half-an-hour'. She described his techniques as 'shadow-judo' and wrote that the sex-offender before him was unaware that the truth is 'about to be torn from his own throat'.

That Ray could lay claim to being at least one step ahead of his client is a dubious accolade. To be one step ahead of a duplicitous sex-offender may not be something to be proud of. How could he understand their mental machinations? What does that say about him? Yet, this seemingly affable, unassuming, approachable teddy bear did just that. That he put that talent to good use saved him from a life of God-knows what.

Indeed the fact that he earned another reputation as a highly-skilled poker player and conjuror affirms his expertise in persuasion and illusion. Ray was a regular visitor to Las Vegas. One hotel used to grant him his own suite of rooms whilst he gambled at their tables. His bank statements showed just why Las Vegas had been so happy to have him. In fact there was a You Tube video of Ray at the gaming tables. He was a paradox, an enigma. But he was damn good at his job. I think if he was 'normal' he wouldn't have been able to do what he did. For that at least we must be truly grateful. Ray was child-like in many ways. His enthusiasm was contagious.

More than once I have heard him described as Machiavellian. He loved that. He was well aware he was capable of being ruthless and that's why he was able to push boundaries and test tolerance. He used it for good — that's why we are now starting to think differently about abusers. That is why we have to read and learn from *MoC*.

Out of all the murderers, rapists and psychopaths Ray dealt with, Robert Black was the one who unsettled him. Ray's remit usually centred around extracting information, challenging distorted beliefs and installing a different mind-set. These men were either in therapy under a probation requirement or being assessed for sentencing. With Black it was a different relationship. He was already serving a prison sentence for the abduction of a little girl. Black, having been aware of Gracewell's work with sex-offenders, had requested that Ray assess him and the report be used in his appeal. He thought that through Ray's findings he would be able to get his sentence reduced. However, on reading the subsequent report, Black withdrew his appeal. He knew it was pointless — Ray knew him better than he knew himself. Robert Black's plan backfired. However, afterwards, Black wanted to take things further — he wanted to continue talking to Ray. So Ray began the exhausting visits to see him in Saughton Prison, Scotland and then later Peterhead Prison there for these sessions. It was unpaid work. Because there was no longer a specific purpose for these meetings, Black opened-up a bit more — shared more about his thoughts and feelings. And Ray was free to ask probing questions in a way that he couldn't normally do in ordinary interviews.

I'm not sure there are many people who would want to listen to a child murderer's ramblings but Ray fell victim to this 'privilege' — he was the only person Black trusted. This is not to say Black confessed to anything or that he was suddenly contrite. Quite the opposite. He went to great lengths to protect himself in these interviews, answering questions in a round-about but revealing way. He was disclosing things rhetorically — using hypotheses rather than being direct. His descriptions were hesitant rather than graphic. They were matter-of-fact not emotional, which made them even more impactive — and to Ray they were more revealing than Black had intended. It was a unique situation.

However, in the descriptions, Ray felt as though Black had taken him into the dilapidated air raid shelter (where one of his earliest attacks had taken place) with him; he could smell the dankness, touch the rough walls and taste the coldness; he could see the little girl, feel her fear, hear her whimper and watch as her unconscious body became floppy and lifeless in front of him as Black squeezed her throat. Ray was unnerved by the experience. These sessions left him exhausted and questioning his own humanity. At times he didn't want to do it. But who else would do it — who else would hear how and what a child killer feels as he is ending the life of a child. Who would want to, anyway?

That Black chose Ray is telling in itself. He saw something in Ray that he trusted. In *MoC* Ray says, 'I have to convince him [Black] that there is nothing he cannot tell me, no part of his mind that we cannot explore safely'. If Ray didn't do it we wouldn't know what Black had to say. And we need to know. We need to know so we can help prevent men like Black turning into men like Black.

I think Ray was incredibly brave to have done what he did. And because he listened to the brutal barbarism of these murders we don't have to. All we have to do is to take on board the lessons and information Ray extracted from Black concerning *how* Black targeted, groomed and operated. We are duty bound to change the way we protect our children.

My fear is that we still won't listen—we still won't learn. We will still choose to stick our heads in the sand. If we don't listen, then apart from losing more children to the Robert Blacks of this world, we will also lose all that Ray unearthed in those interviews. Then, all that Ray endured during those painful sessions would be for nothing.

To counteract these traumatic interviews, Ray injected a vial-full of fun, light entertainment, diversion and distraction into his life. The cinema, snooker, poker, roulette, a doner kebab, paragliding—anything to keep him grounded. He came out of one session then stocked up with hot-dogs, sweets, diet coke and ice-cream and went straight to the cinema to see *Cape Fear* for some light relief. I'm sure though, as he watched Robert de Niro bite into his victim's cheek and Ray bit into his kebab, that Ray was still mulling over the previous three hours with Black. Ray never took himself away from the crusade—his eye was never off the ball. And for that we must give thanks. It was never a question of a bit of me time—'I've had some time-out and now I'll go back to thinking about it'. He was always in it—he lived in the zone. On holiday, sightseeing in Miami meant teaming-up with the police and riding shotgun. True.

Another time in the middle of my birthday weekend away we were about to go down for a nice romantic dinner together. He got a call from the BBC—could they interview him about a high-profile child murder case? Of course they could. When? In the next hour? Certainly. Ray never switched-off. Admirable for the cause—difficult for a wife. This was partly why he flooded our relationship with goodies and treats—to blur the fact that most of the time he wasn't 'there'—even if he was physically present. Again, no matter. The 'cause' needed him more—and without the cause he wasn't Ray Wyre. By his own admission, if you took away his work he wouldn't have an identity. It defined him.

I don't know how he maintained his sunny disposition. He always smiled in the face of adversity. Poker-face for him meant a permanent wry smile. You could read into it whatever you wanted. And whatever you read revealed more about yourself than you intended. That was his 'trick', his art. However, he would reveal little about himself other than what he chose to reveal. That's why he was so proficient with his clients. For them it was like holding up a mirror to themselves. He made them feel that *he knew* what they were thinking. He seemed to know what you were thinking whoever you were.

No matter what chaos or calamity was going on around him (much of it caused by himself) Ray remained the same. For example: The theft and reclamation of his car. I got a call one night after midnight.

'Darling, my car's been stolen — can you come and pick me up?'

'Where are you?'

'Birmingham.'

'Birmingham? Get a taxi. Night, night.'

By now I was painfully familiar with these scenarios. I wasn't being harsh, just practical. He would be home sooner if he got a taxi rather than wait for me to drive all that way. Apparently, he'd left his car running on a petrol station forecourt while he popped in to get a diet coke. In the car he'd left his wallet, house keys, my engraved cigarette lighter (necessity dictated that I smoked), driving licence and his life's work. He watched from the shop as his car was driven away by two men.

Totally unfazed he then tried to blame the station staff because their CCTV cameras didn't serve as a sufficient deterrent and now his car had been stolen as a result! How he got home I can't remember. Three weeks later his car was found and we went to see it in the police compound. This once beautiful silver Vauxhall Omega with its alloy wheels and BMW engine was now an unrecognisable wreck. Windows smashed, tyres slashed, crashed out of all recognition — the inside was even worse. Needless to say everything was gone. I was horrified. Ray surveyed it, unperturbed, with that fixed smile. Then he spotted something glistening on the passenger seat. He reached in through the missing window to pick it up and then declared, beaming with delight as though he'd found a gold nugget, 'Darling! Look! It's your lighter! We've got your lighter!' I looked at him in resigned disbelief at his enthusiasm. So, all wasn't totally lost, then?

Getting such phone calls became less of a surprise to me as time went on. Though he'd phone me about six times a day even when he wasn't away, there was often a 'special' phone call which would require me to do something like fetch a gallon of petrol, find his wallet, passport, keys, phone, a report, etc., etc. Or worse.

'Darling, I've had a bit of an accident.'
'Oh, no! Are you all right?'
'Yes. I'm fine.'
'Where are you?'
'On top of a car. I think it's a Fiesta. I can't tell.'

He'd slid off an elevated section of the road onto the top of a Ford Fiesta which was minding its own business parked outside Tesco's. He wasn't hurt. The AA and Fire Service sorted it all out. Once they'd got his car off the roof of the Fiesta he continued his journey to a conference he was giving in Nottingham. Not shaken, not stirred.

Then there was the time he was attending court for the trial of one of his clients. He parked-up, gathered all his files, etc. and went in. Three hours later the trial was adjourned and he left to come home. He couldn't find his keys. Walking towards the car park he desperately rifled through his pockets. As he approached the car he heard a rumbling sound. It got louder the closer he came to it. Then he realised that the car's engine was still going. For three hours that poor engine had been running, getting hotter and hotter. Not sure what to should do next, Ray calmly opened the unlocked door, climbed into the car — and drove off. What else was there to do? After all he didn't have to start it up. If it hadn't been a diesel it would have blown-up.

Another example shows clearly the benefit of remaining poker-faced. It was whilst Ray was walking through Hammersmith one dark and lonely night. In his arms he was carrying a Diet Coke, burger, sweets, phone, keys and, most precariously, his wallet. Two young men swaggered-up to him. Staring at him in an intimidating fashion they demanded 'Give us your wallet.' Ray looked straight in the eye of the one speaking. 'No,' he replied in a monotone, calm voice. He didn't change his wry Ray expression and continued walking calmly away. And he kept walking at the same pace until he got to the hotel. The two muggers had probably never had that reaction before and must've wondered what was in his arsenal that he could be so confident in declining their request. They decided not to find out. More likely a response they'd usually get was the victim handing over their wallet immediately. They'd never have someone simply say *no*. He was so excited on the phone relating it to me. 'Darling—I've not been mugged!'

CHAPTER 8

Language and Feeling Uncomfortable

During my growth spurt at Luton Rape Crisis Centre there were a couple of incidents in my family's life which I believe would have had totally disastrous or even tragic outcomes had I not started my 'journey' and not brought-up my children to trust their own feelings. Later in this book I explain further why the language we use with children when they are growing-up is so important.

When my son Adam was 12, he and his friend Michael went round our village washing cars. At one job Adam felt uncomfortable with the customer. So did Michael. Finally, job done, the man invited Adam upstairs to look at his Eastern headgear. Then he offered Adam and Michael orange juice. Nothing illegal so far. He gave Adam a ten pound note and said he could return with the change later.

Adam came home and told Pete (we were still together then) and me what had taken place, that they'd felt uncomfortable and that he had to return with the five pounds change. Adam had told us he'd felt uncomfortable, and clearly did not want to go back there. I thanked him for telling us and told him that dad would give this man the change. Pete was not known for his diplomacy and told the man that the reason for him returning the change instead of Adam was that 'there are a lot of weirdos about' and he didn't want Adam coming back there. Strangely, the bloke didn't take offence. That we thought would be the end of the story.

However, this little bloke somehow found out where we lived and came round asking for Adam's help in loading a skip. The answer was a resounding 'No!' of course. Michael, by the way, had said nothing about the car-washing encounter to his parents, when he got home.

I related this odd incident to a colleague at rape crisis. She turned ashen; and asked if this man lived in St Mary's Glebe.

'Yes, he does,' I replied.

'And is his name......?'

'Yes it is'.

Then she told her tragic story of how this same person — a physics teacher at her sons' school — had taken her son 'Paul' under his wing, won the trust of her family, taken him away for a scouting weekend and sexually abused him. Her son didn't tell what had happened to him. He remained silent for four years. It came to light when the school became concerned about his behaviour. He's had counselling but, to date, has issues with his sexuality, relationships and anger control. My son, armed with the word 'uncomfortable' and knowing he'd be believed had told us straightaway.

Although there is more context to this story in terms of creating an environment where Adam felt safe and comfortable enough to tell us of something seemingly trivial, it is a stark example of how bringing-up children to feel empowered, with appropriate tools, in particular accurate language, can and does work. And there's more.

My colleague had reported what had happened to her son, Paul, to the police and the case was taken seriously. They grew an inch-thick dossier on this abuser which I have seen. However, the Crown Prosecution Service (CPS) declared there was 'insufficient evidence' and the case was dropped. It was well-known that RD had been made to leave a private school in Cheshire for inappropriate behaviour towards young boys, but no action was taken. By now he was working at a school in Buckinghamshire. He'd earned the nickname 'Mr Creepy' and the children made fun of him. People in the village, knowing the work I did, would knock on my door now-and-again to inform me that there was yet another middle-Eastern boy living with this man. Though I forwarded the information on to the police, they said there was nothing that could be done legally-speaking.

Sometimes, he would blatantly park his car near the coach stop and watch the boys queuing. Pete once raced him out of the village, tailgating him. The man was brazen about it — untouchable and he knew it. Perhaps, nowadays things might be different and he wouldn't get away with it. I'd like to think he was no longer alive because, if he is still around, for sure he would still be abusing.

Lucy had a close-shave too, at the age of eleven. One morning she'd popped down to the village shop (on the same road) to buy a loaf of bread. Being an aware sort of child, she noticed a red G-reg Maestro car parked on our road. She didn't recognise it and noted its presence. Returning home the car was still there. As she approached, the front passenger door was flung open and the male driver leaned across.

'Hello. Do you know where this lady lives?' he asked, showing her a pornographic magazine picture of a naked woman.

Lucy said nothing but made a run for it and was indoors in a jiffy. Panting and upset, she told me what had happened. She has since told me that she felt totally believed when she fell into my arms.

Later that day, I had the local bobby come round to take a report from her. Not a statement as I didn't want to take anything further. We just wanted it logged: car details, description of the man, time of day etc. If/when he did it again at least it would be on record. I also wanted Lucy to feel believed and confident about telling. Later she told me she had felt totally believed by the grown-ups. We were so lucky to have had such an outcome. Some don't.

At my parents' 40th wedding anniversary party there was a male guest who kept on wanting to dance with the little girls. He took this opportunity to hold and touch them—twirl them around, flirt with them, etc. Two small girls who I knew well looked painfully uncomfortable with him out on the dance floor. Then he came up to Lucy and asked her to dance with him. She said a nice, firm, assertive, 'No thank you' and went on dancing on her own. I was so proud. Whether he was or wasn't unsafe, the fact is Lucy trusted her own feelings and acted on them—whilst still remaining polite of course!

Pick Up the Pieces

CHAPTER 9

Unpacking *The Murder of Childhood*

Once upon a time, almost a generation ago, whenever there was a high-profile sexual-abuse or murder case inciting the uninformed to bay for offenders to be 'locked-up!' and the key thrown away, or that 'They should be castrated!' there was one voice that spoke louder. That voice belonged to Ray Wyre.

'Lock them up and throw the key away?' he'd challenge. 'After serving their sentence they'll be free and angry and *living next-door to you*—with probably more paedophile contacts forged in prison!' 'Castrate a sex-offender? *That* won't stop them hurting children.'

And so he persisted. Ray was never out of the realms of the media. One article referred to him as the 'ubiquitous Ray Wyre'. Be it *Richard and Judy*, *Paxman*, *Woman's Hour* or the *Jeremy Vine Show*, there he was espousing, with clarity and simplicity, his dictum: we need to know how sex-offenders target, groom, abuse and control their environment in order to educate ourselves to be vigilant parents and set victims of abuse free from guilt.

In other words, repugnant though it may be to us, we have to *listen* to what sex-offenders have to tell us. Organizations like Gracewell need the freedom to work with them. Without this information our work with victims is only half done. And our children remain sitting ducks (as already emphasised in *Chapter 8*). I know his seeming obsession with the media prompted remarks, from the narrow-minded and jealous, that he was a 'media whore', but how else could he get his message across? He didn't appear on TV out of vanity or for a bit of fun. His message was clear, concise and consistent. He never turned down an opportunity to comment—to try and educate us. At times I wished he would have.

How I regret that now. I regret it because today, instead of the 'ubiquitous Ray Wyre' popping-up everywhere with his life-saving message delivered with passion and conviction, we have an ominous, eerie silence. We are in the dark and there's no longer that Ray of light.

Whilst I'm certain there are good works being conducted in the world of abuse, there is no consistent, persistent, loud chain-clanking going on in the name of common sense. And this is a tragedy. There appears to be no-one able to take-up the baton and wield it in the face of bigotry and ignorance in the way that Ray did. Consequently, we are alone in the wilderness of abuse.

In re-reading *MoC,* Ray's insightful book written with Tim Tate, I am impressed with its clarity and common sense. Yet I cannot understand why we still choose to remain ignorant and closed to successful methods of dealing with sex-offenders.

I suppose that applying words like: *treatment, listening, understanding, working with, therapy,* etc. when talking about sex-offenders, immediately makes our hackles rise and shuts down our ability to hear. Surely, these words are associated with caring—and shouldn't we just be 'caring' about victims? This misunderstanding is a major obstacle in educating an angry, frightened public. Although, Ray found the public's knee-jerk reaction to horrendous cases understandable at one level, he would never accept that the public could allow that anger to obscure their vision of reality to the detriment of further victims. As his analogy accurately demonstrates, 'Whilst we are rescuing children from the river, no one seems bothered about the man further upstream who's pushing them in.'

Wilful ignorance is at the core of the high prevalence of abuse. If knowledge is power then surely the more we know about sex-offenders the *more* power *we* will have over them—and the *less* power *they will* have. By not listening to them we, quite simply, allow them to hold on to that power. Knowledge is our most effective weapon against sexual-abuse.

Ray was tenacious and determined about his work. With his gentle charm and razor-sharp insight he bravely faced those who opposed him. He was never possessive, competitive or protective about it. The work, Ray believed, should be shared in order for us to learn and move forward. The elaborate conferences he put on—most often just breaking even — were all about spreading the knowledge. It was not about making money! Nowadays there are no more dazzling conferences bringing people together to share their knowledge about sexual child abuse; no more growing the work the Wyre way. In fact the name Ray Wyre is now trademarked so cannot be used without authorisation.

MoC was first published by Penguin Books in 1995 and has now been released in a second and updated edition by Waterside Press, this time with my own involvement alongside Ray's original co-author Tim Tate. It is useful, however, if here in my own book I make certain points and add a few more personal comments, including about how the process of listening to one of the UK's most prolific child serial sex-offenders and serial killers affected Ray himself. *MoC* centres mainly on the interviews Ray conducted with Robert Black a notorious paedophile originally from Grangemouth in Scotland who was convicted of the kidnap, rape, sexual assault and murder of four girls aged from five to eleven between 1981 and 1986 across the United Kingdom, where he travelled in a nondescript white van and with no active check on his whereabouts from managers, family or associates.[1] He was sentenced to life imprisonment, with a recommendation that he serve a minimum tariff of 35 years in prison before becoming eligible to apply for parole, where he died in 2016. His victims represent some of the most high profile child 'vanishings' of all time. They include those of Jennifer Cardy, Susan Maxwell, Caroline Hogg and Sarah Harper. Black was suspected of many more such killings both in the UK and Europe, including that in 1978 of the missing Devon newspaper delivery girl Genette Tate who has never been found, all disappearances that still strike terror into parents and communities everywhere. One of Ray's central theories, in a nutshell, is that sex-offenders will commit offences repeatedly and on an escalating scale whilst devising all kinds of distortions as to what is actually happening and distractions from their true activities.

---

1. Black is one of a number of serial killers who disguised their criminal activities by taking jobs where they enjoyed a measure of unsupervised freedom, usually involving driving and with loose if any checks on their exact whereabouts at any given moment; in an era before modern technology and databases made 'disappearing from the radar' far more difficult. For a survey, see *The Road to Murder: Why Driving is the Occupation of Choice for Britain's Serial Killers,* Adam Lyle, Waterside Press, 2018.

The nationwide manhunt for Black was one of the most exhaustive UK murder investigations of the 20th-century. Each killing makes for a harrowing read. However, the accounts in *MoC* are surprisingly un-sensationalised. There are no gratuitous descriptions of the assaults. But they lay bare the reality of abuse and child murder and its effects. It is a book of considerable integrity that only someone like Ray (with Tim) could write. Indeed, if we allow it to inform us we will be improving child safety. However, our own sensitivities sometimes won't let us even begin to look at what Black told Ray.

How can childhood be murdered—what does that mean? Childhood is murdered when sex abusers take advantage of the upper-hand we have given them and sexually violate a child. Although Black's victims invariably died (but not always), a child doesn't have to die for the murder of her (or his) childhood to occur. A childhood can be obliterated with tragic life-changing consequences without physical death. Black, himself, is a prime example. His beginnings set him on a course that would collide tragically with a stream of little girls. Ray believed sex-offenders are created not born. So, how was the murderer in Robert Black created?

Black's History

Robert Black was born in Falkirk, Scotland in 1947. As he was illegitimate, his mother gave him up for adoption as was not unusual at that time. He was adopted by a couple in their fifties: the Tulips. It appears to have been quite a strict upbringing—strict and lonely. The fact that he did not share their surname drew attention to the fact that he was an orphan. Black knew this and believed that his birth mother hadn't wanted him. He wore thick, strong glasses and often sported bruises about his legs. Living in the rough part of the village, Black earned a reputation of being a bit of a tearaway.

His stepfather, Jack Tulip, died when Black was about five. From then on only he and his stepmother lived alone in the house. He slept in her bed. Punishment often took the form of being hit with a belt across his naked buttocks. One Christmas he received absolutely nothing as he'd been a 'bad boy'. Though many parents may threaten their children with 'Santa won't come if you misbehave' how many of us actually follow through with it? Margaret Tulip did. She was harsh and cruel. He grew up without an ounce of affection or kindness. Interestingly, Black could not remember his stepfather; and no memories at all of life before the age of five. Not one. Ray strongly believed that this was 'unequivocal proof of some early trauma' and that Jack Tulip was involved.

By about eight-years-of age Robert Black had developed a fetish for inserting things into his anus; and covering his hands with excrement. He was interested in orifices and how much he could get inside them. He'd watch as his stepmother wiped herself after she went to the toilet—and he'd already begun playing sexual games with a toddler. He recalled (during his interviews with Ray) an occasion when he was looking after a neighbour's baby—pushing her around in her pushchair. He took her into his house and removed her nappy and 'looked' at her. Ray thought that Black did more than just look. Black was seven when this took place. Given that by now he had an obsession with orifices, it is highly likely that Ray was right. More than 'just looking' must have happened. But looking was all that Black would own up to.

When he was ten Margaret Tulip died and, orphaned a second time, Black was sent to a children's home in Falkirk—that's when the shaping of the rapist and murderer began in earnest.

He was expelled from the children's home and sent to the Red House in Musselburgh. In its early days it had been a 'lunatic asylum'. Then it became a home for destitute boys. The reason for his expulsion from the Falkirk institution was that he had interfered with a young girl in the home. Black was now entering adolescence. Although athletic and interested in football, he had no positive male role model to follow—to show him how to be a man. Instead Black was targeted and sexually abused by one of the home's administrators. This continued for a considerable length of time. He told no-one about it. Why should he? By now feeling like he didn't matter, there was nothing to be gained. He even had to procure new victims for his abuser. Robert Black grew into adulthood never having known what it is to be loved, wanted or valued. This is a fact—a piece of the building block that helped create the murderer—not an attempt to solicit pity or diminish his future behaviour.

During his sessions with Ray, Black revealed a number of occasions where he had abused girls and, in the language he uses to describe these attacks, he sets out to minimise the seriousness of his behaviour and relinquish all responsibility. He even tries to make it look as though the victim participated. In one incident he claimed there was another boy involved:

> 'I don't know who made the approaches. I know it wasn't me because I was called in afterwards and it seemed she'd agreed, for a cigarette, to let us have a look. The girl dropped her knickers and she said "You want to have a look here?" And I just had a look and I think I touched her…I don't know. And then she said, like, she was the boss position, she'd had enough. When she'd had her fag, that was it.'

To an uninformed listener it might sound like juvenile experimentation with no harm done. But, as Ray explains, '… the event was clearly part of a pattern of his life and fitted both with his obsession with under-age girls and with what he called touching their vaginas.' Later on, Black was convicted of a sexual offence involving another young girl. Two similar crimes committed so close together are never insignificant. They show someone on a road that could take him on to murder. But no-one made the link.

It was in June 1963 that Black was convicted of 'lewd and libidinous behaviour' and an assault on a seven-year-old girl, but this description far, far understates what really took place. Black enticed this little girl to go with him to see some kittens. He took her into an old air-raid shelter (needless to say there were no kittens) where he sexually abused her then put his hands around her neck until she went lifeless. Not knowing whether she was alive or dead he continued to abuse her. And there he left her, walking-out into the fresh air not knowing or caring whether she was still alive. The child survived but Black was not tried for attempted murder even though when he'd left her he didn't know for sure whether she was alive or dead. And worse: the juvenile court handed him a deferred sentence for the assault. Was that really all her near-death ordeal was worth?

A report by the Probation Service at the time did in fact state that Black had a 'seriously disturbed personality requiring residential psychiatric care' but this was overlooked. After the trial Black returned to the family he was staying with at the time and as Ray notes, 'His brush with the courts seemed to have instilled a sense of urgency in Black's obsession with children [because] he began repeatedly abusing the young daughter.' But here again, in describing his abuse of the little girl, Black uses language that dismisses the severity of the offence to nothing much. 'I touched a few times... there was once [when] I was actually in bed and she came into the bedroom and laid down on the bed beside me... on top of the covers.' When Ray points out that her so-called compliance was actually behaviour he had programmed himself, Black replies, still trying to blame her, 'I never really invited her into the bedroom before.' No doubt the child would have a different version of these events. An offender's distorted thinking allows him to abuse. It allows him to shift the responsibility onto his victim and is an attempt to protect only himself at all times. It is deliberate, conscious and self-delusional. The tone Black uses in these interviews is light—conversational. There is no gravity at all reflecting the profound severity of what he is relating.

On his rounds as a delivery driver, Black would form 'relationships' as he called them, with young girls who he would eventually sexually abuse. Again it's the distortion and deliberate misuse of language that offenders depend on to diminish their offending. He didn't 'form relationships', he coerced children into believing they were in a relationship/friendship with him in order to win their trust and to confuse them with the intention of sexually abusing them. But it's probably unlikely that they actually felt comfortable with his attentions prior to him abusing them, to even believe that they were in any kind of relationship/friendship at all. Feeling *uncomfortable* would not, in the victim's understanding, amount to danger, given the way we condition children to be polite, etc. And I think it should. The word 'uncomfortable' is a life-saving tool when used in the context of a sound childhood—as my own children had discovered in their close encounters (*Chapter 8*). Children should be brought up to understand and rely on their own feelings rather than defer to us, the adults. When a child feels *uncomfortable* then they're probably right in feeling so.

With his seriously dangerous behaviour remaining unchecked (one of Black's offences had already been dismissed as a 'one-off') Black's offending progressed as might be expected. It remains unknown just when Black started murdering or how many children he murdered or abused. We will never know, now that he is dead — but there were numerous opportunities when this course could have been diverted. Through lack of offender knowledge, they were missed. Tragically, Caroline Hogg, Susan Maxwell and Jennifer Cardy were murdered by Black because he was free to do so. It could also have been the fate of 'Laura Turner' and Teresa Thornhill who were abducted but escaped death.

There are many more murders that fit Black's *modus operandi* but where there was insufficient evidence to prosecute. During the hunt for Susan Maxwell's murderer no one pulled-out Black's name from the local intelligence files. It was later explained that 'Robert Black's record was not serious enough to bring him into the enquiry'.

In March 1964, Black was sent to borstal for one year. It was to be his last custodial sentence for 23 years. It was also the last chance to analyse and influence his pattern of sexual offending. On finishing his sentence Black stayed in a probation hostel in Glasgow. After this, and now with two convictions for sexual offences, he disappeared across the border and headed to London. It was here he lodged with a family who had five boys and two girls. The locals took pity on him and invited him into their homes and families. However, there was something about Black that they were uneasy with and the invitations ceased. It was to do with the way he played boisterously with their children: 'pretend fighting', bouncing them on his knee that made them uncomfortable. He'd been asked to baby-sit them at first but requests for this soon stopped. Black was, by now, a delivery driver with his own van. He practically lived in the van and was pretty much inconspicuous. This allowed him to abduct and abuse undisturbed.

Black's account of Laura Turner's abduction is revealing as it is chilling. The premeditatedness is frightening. From the morning of the abduction, he was determined to abduct a child whilst on his delivery round. There was already one failed attempt that day which was aborted because the conditions 'weren't right': too many people around or the girl had a dog. The external inhibitors were in place. When he saw Laura on her own he parked up and waited. He was prepared. In the van was a sleeping-bag, cushion cover, sticky tape and string. As she approached he grabbed her by the throat and bundled her into the van and drove off. He stopped briefly and, in his own words, 'I pulled her pants to one side and had a look. I thought I'd just sort of stroke her [vagina] … but there was bruising on the inside—I don't know how.' Then he trussed her up with her hands tied behind her back, sealed her mouth with the tape and put the cushion cover over her face. He pushed her into the sleeping-bag and threw her into the corner of the van.

It was only the quick-thinking of a man mowing his lawn that saved six-year-old Laura. What he was witnessing wasn't right: a little girl being bundled, screaming, into a van. He noted the registration number then phoned the police. Instantly, they sprang into action and Black was stopped within minutes. However, what ensued is beyond any parent's worst nightmare.

The officer uncovering the bundle in the back of the van also uncovered his own daughter. She was red and gasping for air. Soon she would have died. That was for certain. I won't even try to imagine his feelings. With this abduction thwarted, Black's murderous reign was finally over. There would be no more Black victims. But it could have been over earlier. Much sooner.

Earlier in 1990, his attempt at abducting Teresa Thornhill had also failed. Though 15 she looked a lot younger in stature and demeanour. Walking home after meeting with a friend, Black shouted across the road to her, 'Oi! Can you fix engines?' She ignored him. Then he strode over, picked her up and tried to bundle her into his van. Teresa struggled, screamed, fought and then bit his hand that he had clamped over her mouth. Black had not anticipated such resistance—and let go. Her friend, on hearing her screams, rushed over and shouted at Black to let her go. Black jumped in the van and took off. Unfortunately, in the dreadful kerfuffle they did not note down the registration number.

Teresa's terrifying ordeal cannot be fully understood or comprehended because all people will think is 'well at least she survived'. Hector Clark, the head of the police investigations, unfortunately confirmed this in his book. He says Teresa 'still lives, unaffected, in Nottingham'.

Given the effect that (my client) Jane's father's behaviour had on her when he 'only' got her to stand in the room whilst he masturbated—Clark's comments show how vital it is to understand, firstly, what constitutes abuse and, secondly, the long-term effects. Although, having a sound childhood and appropriate post-trauma counselling may dilute some of the ensuing effects of such an ordeal, it is doubtful that anyone can live totally 'unaffected' if they have been through what Teresa experienced. And I doubt, if she has children now, that her experience won't have an effect on the way she brings them up.

At all levels as professionals, as parents, as relatives, as friends and neighbours we should make ourselves aware of what sex-abuse is, its effects and, importantly, how we can empower our children and, if abuse does occur, how to reduce the effects.

Throughout his murderous reign, Black maintained that he never wanted his victims to suffer which is why he rendered them unconscious first before taking the sexual abuse to the next level. 'When I tied up Laura I didn't want to actually harm her or hurt her.' This is as ludicrous a claim as it is a lie. In the interview Ray confronts this ridiculous theory: 'but you devastated her. You created so much fear in her... How does abducting a child, tying her hands behind her back, taping her mouth, putting her into a sleeping bag to the extent that she's going to die: how can that *not* be a violent act?' But Black is totally unable to tune into his feelings about this. He uses evasive language and denial all the time. Even when Ray asks him why he can't own-up to the responsibility of what he did, his response is, 'But I was caught before I had really done anything to her.' Ducking and diving the facts all the time. It wasn't a question of him evading the truth because it would be overwhelming for him. It was more that he had nothing to really relate the feeling to. He couldn't imagine, for instance, someone abusing and murdering a son or daughter of his own—or a niece or nephew; because Black had no such relationships in his life so, no, he couldn't relate on a feelings level. He had been brought up without feelings. There could be no sympathy or empathy.

Trying to get Black to *feel* was never going to be possible. He couldn't even feel for himself let alone someone else. He could no more identify with us than we could with him. He had no examples to draw upon. There was no anchor. We feel for his victims because we imagine what it would be like if it happened to our loved ones and that is too painful to countenance. Black couldn't do this. As Ray once observed—when we feel nothing, we can do *anything*. In other words when we have nothing to relate to we are void of feelings. When we're void of feelings there is nothing to stop us doing anything at all. There's no fear, no red flags or warning markers in place to stop us going over the precipice. Punishment rarely acts as a deterrent. It just helps us to further shut down from positive feelings. Punishment begets anger.

All his life Black lived without feelings and emotions. He was empty of these. But he would not have started out like this. He would have begun life with the capacity to love and accept love intact. Bit by bit it was eroded by his life experiences: his continual rejection—from his natural mother to a short-lived engagement (about which nothing more is known). Pushed from pillar to post and being grossly sexually-abused along the way and down the road to this fatal abyss. Nobody wanted him in their lives. Then there were the lost opportunities when the powers that be allowed him to slip through the net time-and-time-again. It is not unreasonable to say that it is society that failed *him*. And society has paid the price for that failure. In particular, of course, the parents of the murdered girls.

Probation, juvenile courts, care systems all failed to see the bigger picture. Would it have been a different story had any of these institutions had abuser knowledge? Could there have been a different outcome had some of his un-murdered abuse victims been brought-up to trust their own feelings and had not had to be polite and obedient? With everything in place, i.e. had Black received therapy for his behaviour and distorted thinking early on; had Black been loved by his adoptive parents; had his engagement given him the love and security he craved; had he felt valued as a human being; had he not been sexually abused as a child himself, then it is highly unlikely we would have had this multiple child murderer in our midst. His distorted behaviour was born out of a distorted life. Black murdered the childhoods that he realised he hadn't had when he was a boy; jealousy for sure played a part in it.

His murderous behaviour does not evoke empathy. How could it? We all feel utter revulsion not only towards it but towards him as a person. He is a monster, a pervert, an animal—we hate him, we want to hate him because we cannot find anything in him that we can relate to. He is not like us. We distance ourselves from him (and men like him) as far as possible because we can't accept that this human being was capable of doing what he did. We alienate him to protect ourselves. He is *other* than human. By de-humanising him we feel safe—united in our hatred. We do not want to understand how he came to exist, probably because we might find something of ourselves within him—something recognisable. And that is too abhorrent to contemplate.

It is untrue to say that a childhood like Black's *will* result in a murderer. It is not a mathematical equation. After all there are many people who have had similar loveless childhoods who might also have been sexually abused who have not become rapists or murderers of children. But Black's childhood was a contributing factor as indeed were all the missed chances to address his escalating behaviour. However, it is also short-sighted and does not help us do something positive in the name of child-protection. As Ray says:

> 'Only we as a society can begin to protect our children from those whose desire is to abduct, abuse or kill them. But to do that requires understanding; understanding brought about by a willingness to work with those whom we call "monsters" and to learn the lessons they have to teach us.'[2]

What *MoC* tells us is that we have to *allow* work with sex-offenders to take place. And not under the cover of darkness either—but in broad daylight. In other words we have to accept that this work needs to be done and allow it space within our communities. We are extremely lucky that there are people out there who want to and are able to take this

---

2. *MoC*. See the Introduction to that work.

work on. We should be hugely grateful that they exist because whilst they do the work, we don't have to. All we have to do is to give them the space in which to do it—un-hindered and un-persecuted. I certainly wouldn't be able to work with abusers. It takes a special kind of person to work directly with them. But I want to know what these incredible people have gleaned from their abusing clients so I can improve my own knowledge of how abusers operate. So, when *MoC* suggests we listen to sex offenders it means listening to those who work with them. It doesn't mean chatting to a paedophile down the pub. We as a society have a moral obligation to support these therapists—it is no easy job.

Key Pointers

We as adults refuse to learn a better way of protecting our children and we allow murderers and sex-abusers the upper-hand. And this is what happens when that upper-hand is taken and a child is sexually abused. So, *MoC* tells us:

- **The majority of abusers cannot abuse without our help.** Without the way we condition children, abusers would find it far more difficult to abuse.

- **We do not want to listen to abusers.** Those of us who don't want to hear are precisely the reason why our children are vulnerable. As Ray says, 'It is as though only by remaining wilfully ignorant could a community feel safe.'

- **Knowledge is power.** So why do we choose not to know and prefer to remain powerless? We live in a society that is content to let offenders hold onto their distorted beliefs. We can reduce their power by increasing our knowledge.

- **Hatred of abusers is a luxury we cannot afford.** It is blind, short-sighted and dangerous. It is, quite simply, the murder of childhood.

Pick Up the Pieces

CHAPTER 10

Farewell to Gracewell: Goodbye Common Sense

The Gracewell Clinic which I briefly introduced in *Chapter 1* acted as a highly effective filter system for us, the public. It siphoned-off information divulged by sex-offenders and turned it into knowledge through which we could protect our children. Gracewell was open to public scrutiny. It was transparent. Gracewell had nothing to hide—no secrets. But alas, the Nimbys won. And what a hollow victory it was for them. The closing of Gracewell was and is heartbreaking. In *MoC*, Ray describes it as follows:

> 'Just after we closed our door, I heard the sound of an explosion in the porch. I went to investigate and was greeted by a wall of flames. With another colleague we managed to extinguish the fire and walked through the charred woodwork to look outside. I walked over to the man standing watching us with a petrol can in his hand. He claimed triumphantly that it was his handiwork. "There was perverts in there". I told him that we only had mothers and children that afternoon (non-abusing partner work) and invited him inside. As we waited for the police to come and arrest him I made him a cup of coffee and tried to explain the real work of Gracewell. But of course, by now, it was all over. Their successful campaign to close Gracewell was in motion. This man was just putting the finishing touches to it.
>
> On Wednesday 29th December 1993 I locked the heavy green door of 25–33 Park Road [Birmingham] for the last time. I was walking away from a major part of my life. We had been accountable to the relevant authorities for all aspects of the service. We had already had the approval of Whitehall.

But whilst the professionals were happy to accept us, the local community was not. In a way our success and growing public profile fomented a degree of controversy among those who believed that treating sex offenders is wrong. In spite of all the plaudits from police, probation officers, social services and the courts and even the Home Office a handful of residents began a campaign to force the clinic away from their streets. It was born out of misinformation and blind prejudice.'[1]

It would appear the local residents would much prefer to have offenders living anonymously in the community, unsupervised and untreated. Ironically, the day Gracewell closed the men simply went out into the community from whence they came — bedsit accommodation in Birmingham itself — probably next-door to a Nimby. How safe would that have made the community? 'It was quite simply, madness,' said Ray. By closing Gracewell the residents 'did not protect one more child. In fact, the reverse is true: they put children at risk.' The council did paedophilia's work for it. A sex-offender in treatment hugely reduces his risk of re-offending. As Gracewell's records showed. Wilful ignorance is wholly to blame for the closing of Gracewell. It's as though clinging to their ignorance people believe they are safe. Quite the opposite is true.

Gracewell was our only defence between us, the uninformed public, and *them,* the abusing population. Through their findings we could learn how to protect our children whilst abusers were challenged and made to confront their own distorted beliefs. The campaign to close Gracewell was a grossly irresponsible act. The attitude of the campaigners still permeates society today to the detriment of our children and is a triumph for abusers.

As with most crimes and criminals we seek to find out why and how a person can commit a particular offence. We want to understand so we can protect ourselves, change their thinking and prevent it happening again. There are programmes set-up to rehabilitate offenders of most

---

1. *MoC.* Original 1995 Epilogue as reproduced in the 2018 Waterside Press edition. Note that whilst policing remains an overall responsibility of the Home Office, justice-related function such as courts, sentencing, prisons, probation and sex-offender treatment programmes now fall under the Ministry of Justice.

crimes: burglary, violence, car-theft, fraud, etc. We listen because we want to understand—to help. But this is not the case with sex-offenders.

Although Robert Black went way beyond being *only* a sex-offender, it may have been possible to stop him before he became a *murdering* sex-offender. In all the cases where he tried to 'create' a relationship with the child before abusing her, Black would have targeted a particular kind of child. One who was accessible, vulnerable, easy to isolate, ripe to corrupt. He made himself approachable to children in order to win their trust and would have made himself easy to engage with. He would have been easy to talk to. But at some point that would have changed into something quite out of the child's comfort zone. It is highly unlikely that any of his abuse victims would have wanted the situation to progress to touching.

Having taken things to a 'touching' level, how did he secure their silence? For example, the children of the people he was staying with. The abuse happened on more than one occasion. Yet he was confident enough to let children go after he'd abused them, back to the family fold. In *MoC* we don't hear from the victims who got away (i.e. the girls he 'befriended' on his delivery rounds whom he says he touched) as to how they felt, coped and whether they told but for sure none of them would have gone along with what Black had done to them. Their accounts of their experiences would sound nothing like Black's.

The Two-way Mirror

On one of our visits to Gracewell, my colleagues and I observed a group therapy session through the two-way mirror. We could see them but they couldn't see us. It was the turn of 'Eric' to stand up and talk about his abuse of a ten-year-old boy whom Eric had been accused of abusing at his flat. The allegation was that Eric had 'fondled' the boy and tried to masturbate him. He had denied the allegation. I think he was at Gracewell to be assessed. Eric stood up. He was a large man, his hair thinning on top. With his bulbous fingers he picked-up the felt pen and began writing on the flip-chart. First his name, then he began explaining why he was there—from *his* perspective. It went something like this:

> 'I'd seen "Steven" [the boy] in the slot-machine arcade [at the fair]. I'd seen him a couple of times there. He needed change so I offered him some coins so he could continue playing. The next day he was there too. He smiled at me. I felt sorry for him because he was on his own. We got chatting. When I asked him where his parents were he said they were at home — drunk. I got the impression he didn't have a happy home life.
>
> One day soon after, Steven was there at the arcade and looked very upset. I took him for a coke and something to eat as he was hungry. We got close. He was saying horrible stuff about his parents and I tried to get him to understand that it's difficult being a parent.'

Eric was contextualising the relationship, in the way he wanted everyone to see it. But he forgot he was addressing a group of sex-offenders like himself who knew what he was trying to do — and that was to come across as a caring man who just wanted to help, not a praying mantis working on his victim. They could see through his lies. 'You were grooming him,' called out one, confronting Eric's motives. The clients at Gracewell quickly picked-up the jargon when in therapy. 'No. I genuinely felt sorry for him.' Eric was not believed.

> 'I asked him if he'd like to come back to my flat — he was in a terrible state — upset about his parents. I just wanted to help. But he said no. And that was fine. A couple of days later I saw him out in the park, again all alone. We got chatting again. He'd heard of *Ghostbusters* but hadn't seen the film. So, I invited him to come over the following day to watch the video — which he was quite comfortable to do. I cleaned the place up, bought some éclairs and waited for him. So we sat and watched the film together. Steven came and sat next to me with a plate full of éclairs and a coke. Half way through the film he began to feel sick. I'd forgotten that he said he couldn't eat dairy products. I rubbed his tummy to ease the pain. My hand slipped and I accidently brushed against his genitals. That was all. He never complained; never said a word. He just sat there — I didn't think he'd even noticed. He certainly didn't say anything to me at the time. But then

he went home and complained to his parents. The next thing I know the police are knocking on my door accusing me of abuse!'

Now it was the group's turn to 'unpack' Eric's story. In fact they totally dismantled his version and rebuilt it.

Firstly they challenged why he was loitering around a fairground, they didn't believe he just 'came across' the boy in the park by chance — he actually went looking for him. When he said it was 'fine' that the boy declined his first invitation to Eric's flat — he was 'fine' about it because he wanted to win the boy's trust. And when he said he'd 'forgotten' the boy had an allergy to dairy products, he hadn't forgotten. In fact he deliberately bought éclairs to make the boy feel sick so he would need 'comforting'. And as for the boy 'feeling comfortable sitting next to Eric' — it turned out that there was only one large chair in the room. There was nowhere else for him to sit but with Eric. That was deliberate.

The robust confrontation between Eric and the group finally exposed Eric as a premeditated, fixated paedophile whose sole motive was to sexually abuse the boy (or boys). Eric had been patient — abusers often are — in order to capture his prey. Trying to maintain that the assault was an accidental slip-of-the-hand — and that nothing like that had ever happened before — didn't hold water with his peers. Eric was exposed by his own kind who knew his motives, recognised his *modus operandi* and dismissed his plea that it was accidental or a one-off.

This session was amazing to watch. Being dispossessed of his distorted beliefs and lies was only the beginning for Eric. And if I'd thought before that Gracewell was a soft option compared to prison for these sexual deviants, then I was happily proved completely wrong. There were many Erics in Gracewell. Even more of them out there living amongst us — totally protected by our ignorance.

If Steven's parents had brought him up not to speak to strangers then it is important to note that a stranger can become a friend within seconds. For a child, a simple 'Hello' turns a stranger into a 'friend'. It is ironic, too, that about the time I was setting-up the self-help group in Hemel Hempstead there was a child-safety video being shown to schoolchildren of around the age of five to seven all about being able to say 'No'.

It addressed the issue of inappropriate touching and defined the 'no-go' areas of a child's body. All admirable stuff. In fact they'd turned saying 'No' into a bouncy little ditty—'We can say no, I can say no, you can say no' dum-de-dum-de-dum, etc. The presenter was Rolf Harris

Convicted abusers constantly claim their offending was a 'one-off'. This is rarely the case. Ray:

> 'At Gracewell our inclination was never to accept unquestioningly what an offender told us.'

Therefore when an offender claims it was a 'one-off' it is unlikely to be the case. Investigating abusers' masturbatory fantasies often reveals evidence that a so-called one-off is a culmination of abusive fantasies. However, because society punishes more harshly those who plan their offending, abusers have an investment in trying to convince the courts that their offence was 'just a one-off'. Fantasies of sexual abuse too often progress to becoming reality. Although we all make fun of the park flasher, the chances are he is on a continuum. When flashing no longer gives him the buzz he once got, what will he do next to find it?

De-frocked Priests and Other Distortions

At one point there were so many defrocked priests at the Gracewell Clinic that I, as a (former) Catholic, was left totally confused. When I entered the premises I felt I ought to genuflect and say, 'Bless me father but *you* have sinned …' as I made the sign of the cross. I fully expected a small font of holy water by the entrance and a statue of Our Lady to appear sooner or later. It was disconcerting. But if you're an abuser it makes sense to join a respected organization for protection. Except now with so many high-profile clerical cases it seems the priesthood was (and maybe is) rife with child abusers—though I hope that's not the case

Of course, there are many well-known cases of the clergy sexually-abusing children in their care. One parish I lived in was rife with allegations and accusations of sex abuse.

In 2009, for instance, one man was jailed for eight years for sexually assaulting boys whilst he was a priest there. Shockingly, he is the fifth to date to be accused. Reportedly, one ten-year-old victim of his had tried to hang himself after the man 'fondled' him. And though this priest was investigated in 2001 and again in 2004, no charges were brought. My cousin was a pupil of his earlier in the man's career and has commented that he always felt uncomfortable in his company—and was obviously relieved his teacher didn't take a shine to him during his time at school.

Another man, Father A, who had been the headmaster and abbot there during the 1990s was accused of abusing several boys during his term in charge. One of his alleged victims has described his ordeal of being molested frequently in Father A's office as being the source of horrendous nightmares. His reasons for remaining silent were that he knew he wouldn't be believed, he was embarrassed and thought he would get beaten. That he wouldn't be believed is probably how and why abuse by clergy is so prevalent.

Abuse by those enjoying such a position of trust, will always be met with more astonishment and anger than that against 'normal' abusers as it does call into question just how many members of the clergy are drawn to the priesthood because of the trust bestowed on them by us and are therefore protected and free to behave as they choose. Such men-of-the-cloth want to be seen as above suspicion. But that is fast becoming a thing of the past. Nowadays the clergy are becoming more and more synonymous with sexual abuse and the church is doing itself no favours in its response to abuse cases. For instance relocating Father A just fuels the accusation that the church seems ever-ready to cover-up and turn a blind-eye. This is done under the guise of 'forgiveness' and the belief that sinners should be given a second chance.

More recently the Catholic hierarchy (in Scotland) has protected yet another priest by sending him off to North America for 'treatment'. And worse, the bishop didn't inform police for eight months after the priest concerned admitted having abused boys in his care. In a statement the church said it wished to 'sincerely renew its apologies to victims'. Apologies are easy to make and are in no way a means of accepting responsibility. They also require 'forgiveness' in response. However, I believe there can only be forgiveness when there has been true contrition. And this is why there were so many priests at Gracewell Clinic. They were there to look at their behaviour with honesty and begin to take true responsibility without cutting straight through to the end bit of forgiving themselves.

One Catholic priest residing at Gracewell was, on the face of it, the epitome of the 'good priest'. One whom, even I with abuser knowledge and experience, would have struggled to accept as an actual abuser. He had rounded, soft features. Not perfect but that only added to his kindly appearance. He was softly-spoken and would look with honesty into your eyes as he spoke — head tilted to one side. Father B was avuncular, approachable and gentle. Yet here he was being apprised of his distorted thinking, his heinous behaviour was being challenged by other offending clergy, as he looked lost and forlorn. One could even feel sorry for him. Father B had been a respected counsellor, a supporter for many years of one particular family of Irish descent. Weddings, baptisms, funerals, last rites, he was there for them night or day. He was practically part of the family. But all this was just a ruse to cover-up his real motive and that was to sexually-abuse the family's youngest daughter.

'Kathleen' blurted it out at the wake for her beloved father. She was now 14. The abuse had begun when she was six. Her allegations were taken seriously and Father B volunteered for treatment at Gracewell Clinic which was paid for by the Catholic Church. Whether it all ended 'happily ever-after' no one knows. His stay at Gracewell was only for six months. Six months to undo 64 years of distorted thinking. That's quite a task; but I know Gracewell would have achieved more in changing his attitude than six months in jail ever would.

Survival

Sadly, as abuser behaviour is misinterpreted, e.g. believing a perpetrator when he says his offence is a one-off, then so too is victim behaviour misunderstood in court. Whilst courts seem more comfortable in accepting a perpetrator's story, victims on the other hand tend to be treated as liars. Victim behaviour is, at the core, survival behaviour and there are many examples where, intent on surviving rape/sexual abuse, a victim will do anything to survive.

A case in point was a client of mine 'Sarah' who got chatting to a man in a pub. Her friend had already left and, when Sarah got up to leave to go home, he offered to walk with her as her protector. He had won her trust though in hindsight she did admit to feeling uncomfortable when he had made the 'gallant' offer, but she'd felt it rude to decline. As they walked by a field he grabbed her by the hair, dragged her into the field and began attacking her. She thought he was going to kill her. Trying to keep 'on his side' and fearing his anger, she pretended to go along with it. Talking in a calm voice trying not to show how terrified she was. She even undid her own blouse to avoid the violent act of him ripping it off her which she knew that, in his rage, he was capable of doing. But she wanted to live—that is all she focused on. On leaving he warned her to stay put as he would be watching her and would return to slit her throat if she moved.

So there she remained until the early hours when a police patrol car picked her up. Her story, told factually in her statement, didn't even reach the Crown Prosecution Service. Insufficient evidence and what evidence there was could easily have been dismissed as showing consensual behaviour, albeit rough sex: she'd been seen chatting with him, had left willingly with him, there had been no apparent struggle (not even a ripped blouse), she'd had a drink, she hadn't left the scene. In her bid to survive, everything she'd done to avoid death and protect herself would go against her.

A few years ago a project was set up dealing with rape and sexual abuse. Part of this programme looked at ways in which a woman can survive rape 'better'. In it they dared to suggest that, often in rape cases, lack of evidence that could identify the rapist was the weak factor in a successful prosecution. It was suggested that evidence can be gained during the attack by trying to obtain sources of DNA, such as hair, blood or saliva. In doing this a woman can feel that she is taking back some of the control. It has proved successful in a couple of high profile cases. The victims felt that gleaning evidence helped them focus on survival rather than leaving them feeling totally defeated. This survival behaviour was challenged as others felt it shifted the responsibility onto the victim. However, there is a place for looking at this — certainly if it means improved survival prospects in the aftermath.

In childhood abuse, survivor behaviour of the child in trying to make sense of senseless abuse will confuse those who do not understand real survivor behaviour.

'Sally' (a client of mine) used to go to her father for sex on a Friday evening before he went out for the evening. Why? Because what usually happened on a Friday night was he would roll in drunk in the small hours, go to his bedroom and try to have sex with Sally's mother. She would reject his drunken advances and kick him out of bed. So off he'd go to Sally's room, wake her up and sexually abuse her, finally progressing to raping her when she was older. In offering him sex before he went out, Sally avoided the violent rape she would be subjected to later and, in her own way, by 'offering' him sex she felt she had taken back some power and control over the situation. That's survival behaviour.

Maybe a judge and jury today would see it as such but whilst ever judges make astounding declarations like, 'She was no angel' implying that a nine-year-old girl had sexual knowledge beyond her years and therefore partly to blame, then victim behaviour will continue to be misunderstood. And whilst defendants' lawyers use that behaviour knowledge in their defence strategy surely today we should realise that promiscuous behaviour (of a child) is the result of a sexually-abusive, corrupted relationship. And that a child should never share even part of that blame.

How, for instance, would my own behaviour in relation to my grandfather (described in *Chapter 3*) have appeared in court, especially at that time? She accepted money, sometimes she'd ask for money even when she knew he was poor. Didn't she go willingly to his room? Why didn't she tell anyone? Didn't she like it sometimes? I think as a child I sensed all would go disastrously for me if I told. My experience of being believed by my parents was not a good one. From a broken vase to nicking the neighbour's tulips, my innocence was always questioned. The argument against me was too great — and I knew, as soon as I opened my mouth, I wouldn't be believed. Keeping silent gave me a semblance of control of the situation. How far have we moved on from seeing victim/survivor behaviour as being compliant? Probably not very far.

Robert Black was a 'seductive' paedophile which means that he would attempt to form a 'relationship' with his victim purely to abuse them. And he actually wanted to believe he formed relationships with these children. Or rather he had an investment in making himself believe this. He chose not to feed himself the facts, for example, that a child would feel terrified having hands placed around her neck and squeezed. How can anyone believe otherwise? Even Black? How remote from his feelings would he have to have been to be able to make himself believe this trough of lies. And what language did he use to justify his behaviour to himself whilst squeezing a child's throat? And how on earth can he believe he could convince the world that he throttled a child into unconsciousness for her own good—because 'I didn't want to hurt her'? To say Black was mad just evades the issue and keeps him separated from being human. He was not mad. He was a man who chose to sexually abuse and murder.

Abused Abusers, Red-herrings and Listening to Voices

Sexual abuse is the overpowering of a perceived insignificant person (e.g. a child/a woman) using sex as the weapon to gain this power. An abused boy might, as he becomes an adult, see that abusing a child recovers that power. Hence the majority of offenders in treatment claim to have been abused in childhood themselves thus perpetuating the cycle of sexual abuse. However, this is no excuse. An adult abuser makes an informed choice to abuse. Ray never allowed an abuser's own abuse story to overshadow offender work. It would be addressed separately after offender issues were challenged.

Another red-herring in an abuser's *modus operandi* is that of altruism. Abusers need to be seen as nice in order to gain our trust. In trying to be nice, an abuser will carry-out good deeds, be helpful and kind, become a pillar of society so as to achieve 'niceness' and respectability. And just to confuse things further, another side of them is also genuinely wanting this good side to be true. They want to prove to themselves that they're not wholly bad. Part of the task of therapists, then, is to identify what part of 'nice' is true and what part is just a devious ruse. Would we, the general public, know how to differentiate? Of course not. That is why therapists working with offenders are so vital to us. They know what to look for and how to go about it — *so we don't have to!*

Ray's interviews with Robert Black do show us, however, the power of language and how it influences us. In fact in order to change behaviour, feelings, thoughts and beliefs we have to first employ *language*. This is important to remember. Words control everything. Having an adequate vocabulary and using it accurately puts us in control of language. When my own negative composite voices controlled me I struggled to develop a positive language to counteract them. But gradually I realised that these negative voices were not being honest.

I wasn't an arse, nor was I stupid or weak or ineffective. All that was simply lies. In reality I am strong, insightful, capable and more. I had to claw back the power they wielded. At first it felt quite strange to apply these positive words to myself. But, in a sense, it was also easy to apply them because they were true — unlike the other voices. Slowly these positives became stronger and louder the more I used them. And more often than not they would defeat the negative ones that battled for control. I'm not saying they're completely gone — but they're a lot, lot quieter. And I know how to shut them up. Because these voices were recorded in childhood, they form part of my hard drive and as such will probably always remain there. I accept this. But as an adult armed with better knowledge, I can now make informed choices as to which voice I listen to: the negative ones or the positive ones. On the occasions I choose the negative voices I forgive myself and move on. It's a matter of persistence and perseverance. *Letting go* lies and *letting in* the facts.

Martin

One Gracewell case was that of the man found guilty of abusing his stepdaughter. His grooming method was characteristically devious. Where once 'Martin' wanted everyone to believe he had carelessly left a pornographic video lying around, it turned out, in therapy, this was a sexual fantasy come to fruition.

Martin met his wife, 'Sue', through a dating agency. She had two daughters aged eight and 13—but he 'didn't mind'. He had a daughter of his own, so knew what to expect. He seemed to adore Sue and became very accepting of his new charges. After a while Martin and Sue married and everything was bliss. Sue mainly worked nights and left the house at six to get to the hospital where she worked as a nurse. Martin was happy to cook for the girls every evening. 'Emma' the younger one, was always packed-off to bed early. Left alone with 'Jenny' all evening he became her confidante. Mum was always too busy, she never listened, never allowed her any freedom—so Jenny would pour out her heart to Martin.

Gradually he began to introduce the idea of sex education. Talking vaguely at first about rabbits and progressing to 'mums and dads' revealing a little bit as to why he and their mum shared a bed. Most evenings would also involve a bit of horseplay with the girls. Once Emma had gone to bed Jenny, being the older, was allowed to watch 'grown-up' programmes with a 'Don't tell mum' caveat attached. On Fridays Jenny was allowed to stay up late and choose a video to watch. She inevitably would choose one that she knew her mum would not approve of—but it was *their little secret*. The choice of videos made available to her represented an increasing amount of sexual content.

Then one evening, Martin deliberately left some extreme pornographic videos, with dubious titles, lying about. With her curiosity roused but believing Martin wouldn't really approve, Jenny snuck the tape into the machine and started watching. Martin, knowing what she'd done, waited a good long while before striding into the sitting-room feigning anger.

'What are you watching?' he demanded accusingly, knowing full well what Jenny been watching.

Jenny knew she'd been caught and reacted with obvious embarrassment. But Martin had achieved what he'd set out to. He'd been watching her through the crack in the door enjoying seeing her looking at the sexual acts on screen. And now she felt guilty. He'd got her exactly where he wanted her: feeling embarrassed and guilty—and completely dependent on him. He promised not to tell Sue and allowed the noxious secret to do its work.

Jenny became difficult with her mum. Rebellious. But Martin was always there to smooth things over. 'You always take her side,' Sue would complain. But this was just a ruse. He made himself look good in Sue's eyes because, whilst showering Sue with affection, Sue believed he was just trying to be a good understanding step-dad. And she appreciated that. She also blamed herself for not being more patient with Jenny. However, Martin then began pointing-out things about Jenny to Sue: she doesn't do her homework, she doesn't do her chores, she picks on Emma. All these 'observations' were 'leaked' to Sue who then became more exasperated with Jenny.

Bit-by-bit Martin alienated mother and daughter. He isolated Jenny and then moved in on her sexually. It started with him comforting her when they were alone, after she'd had a blazing row with her mum. Using flattery and 'understanding' he slowly but surely made himself the only one Jenny could turn to. And with Jenny developing an attraction towards Martin, being on the cusp of puberty, he was assured of her silence. How could she possibly tell her mother what was really happening? Sue loved him. He was generous. Jenny loved her mum — but she could no longer reach her. She was also becoming jealous of Sue's relationship with Martin.

Home life had become impossible for all — except Martin. He was in control of everyone. His odious plan unravelled after a couple of years when Emma found Jenny and Martin 'doing things'. After a long, painful and protracted investigation he was successfully charged with under-age sex — hence his residence at Gracewell. Men like Martin target women like Sue. It is the children Martin was after — not her. There were three victims in this case and no winners.

CHAPTER 11

Jane and Maureen

Jane: 'Do I Qualify to Join this Group?'

I'll never forget this question, which I was asked during my time at the Hemel group. 'Jane' was 30-something. She asked tentatively before coming into the meeting room whether she 'qualified'. I took her to a quiet room, made her a cup of tea. We sat down and I gently asked what she meant. Our conversation went more or less like this:

> 'Well, my father never laid a finger on me. Ever. He and my mum had separated before I was four so I didn't know him that well. But when I turned six I had to go and stay with him at the weekends. Right from day one he asked me to stay in the toilet with him when he went for a wee. That was the first time I'd seen a penis. He told me to look while he went. I remember being shocked and very embarrassed. After a couple of weekends with him I told my mum I didn't want to go there anymore. She didn't ask me why but I still had to go.'

> 'Did you tell her what had been happening?'

> 'No. Stupid really, because it felt rude! Then one morning he called me into his bedroom. He was standing there, naked. He asked me to take off my nightie. I remember being frightened. Then he started to masturbate whilst looking at me. He made these horrible noises. Moments later he ejaculated. And that was that. It happened a few times after that. But that was all. He

never touched me. I never had to touch him either. At least he never made me do that.'

I have since met quite a few Janes—women who feel they have to grade their abuse for it to count. What had taken place in Jane's life was ghastly. She hardly knew her dad—when she had to stay with him she was actually staying with a stranger. Up until that point she could recall no relationship with him. But all of a sudden she had to trust him—because he was an adult and another adult had said so. She didn't know how to protect herself or who to turn to. Jane avoided telling her mother thinking, 'What's wrong with me?'

'She didn't make it okay for me to tell, somehow. I wouldn't have known how to say it anyway. I was embarrassed.' So Jane's secret festered away. And she asked herself the same questions I'd asked myself at around that age—what did I do? The unspoken answers to those questions eat away at a child's self-worth, so she 'naturally' takes the blame. In a bizarre way taking the blame allows her a level of control. And similarly, as in my case (and others), Jane began to internalise her feelings. Over time she turned her anger onto herself. By the time Jane was ten she was self-harming. Cutting her arms (the marks could be hidden under sleeves) pulling chunks of her hair out and comfort-eating. School work, too, suffered. Her mum was worried. But the more her mum worried and probed the worse Jane felt.

For a powerless abused child to tell is to expose her own degradation and humiliation and insignificance with no assurance of a positive response from whoever she is telling. Why on earth would an abused child tell? I'm surprised we ever tell even when we grow-up. It is humiliating even though by then we know it wasn't our fault. Knowing it wasn't our fault and *feeling* it wasn't our fault are two entirely separate things.

Jane, when she came to our group, had struggled with alcohol, eating disorders and had had two broken relationships. She couldn't allow herself to enjoy a healthy sexual relationship. It felt dirty. But, as time went on and she attended the meetings, she experienced empowerment as I had done in my trips to the Essex group: she felt believed and no longer alone.

So, sexual abuse does not have to involve physical contact for the same effects to foment. It would appear though that women are more likely to internalise the effects, i.e. we take it out on ourselves. Self-harming, eating disorders, drug-taking, etc. Women tend to repress their anger within themselves which often results in depression. Anger always finds a way out. I believe my tonsillitis as a child was a direct response to what was happening to me; suppressing it only meant it found another escape route.

Sexual abuse is the taking away of power and control by someone in a 'superior' position to the victim. It is using sex as the weapon to gain that control. Sometimes the child's own sexuality is used as well, i.e. getting a child's body to respond. Keeping and maintaining the secret destroys the very core of a child — her/his very soul. So how on earth can we expect a sexually-abused child to grow-up healthy in body, mind and soul? Feeling as she does — second rate — how will she make the right decisions given her low self-esteem? The chances are she/he won't. Accepting second best becomes second nature to her. And with a corrupted view of sex, how will she enter into a healthy relationship. If she believes sex is merely a commodity it is no wonder 90 per cent of sex workers come from sexually abusive childhoods. Sex becomes a means of earning a living — or given in the hope of receiving love in return.

However, some people survive sexually-abusive childhoods better than others. How? There are many elements to this and, again, it is not a mathematical equation. I believe, though the actual acts of what happened to me seemed more severe than Jane's, I survived better. This is because there were other factors at play. I loved my mum and I felt loved enough by her. I did everything I could to hold on to that love, i.e. being a good girl. I was terrified that, if I behaved badly, then I would lose that love. That belief kept me on the straight and narrow because the underworld fascinated me and I so wanted to go to it. I was drawn to it and felt I belonged there. It was familiar to me.

Now at that point had there been someone out there eager to exploit me, then for sure it would have happened. Without a doubt. However, I was scared of descending to the dark side no matter how seductively it beckoned me. I was scared because I would lose mum's love. Controlling though she was, disappointed in me though she was, it was still only because of her that I survived in the end. Her and my music teacher. Miss Peskett taking an interest in me navigated me away from the rocks to safe waters. My guitar became a healthy distraction and a wholesome obsession. I consider myself lucky. I know I was fortunate to have survived a traumatic childhood and to be where I am today.

In Jane's case she did not have any kind of rescuing relationship in her life. She didn't feel loved and didn't have a close relationship with her mum. She was also an only child. No kind music teacher looked favourably on her unfortunately, so Jane was allowed to slip into despair and used destructive 'coping' methods until she came to the group. However, through attending the group, she rescued herself. She took back her power. Power that is given still belongs to the person giving it. Power has to be taken. Jane took her's back.

Maureen: Finding Solace

'Maureen' on the other hand, had experienced a violent childhood. Briefly, her story was: her father had returned from the war a very angry man resentful of his ten children. He picked Maureen to be his 'favourite'. He raped her frequently, punched and kicked her around, eventually breaking her arm. Her siblings never stepped-in but she felt they were relieved because whilst he was laying into to her he wasn't picking on them. She'd go to school in soiled clothes and smelled terribly. Needless to say Maureen was bullied — as if things weren't bad enough. At the age of 12 Maureen ran away from home but, incredibly, was returned by the police who believed everything her father told them. Predictably the abuse escalated, if that was possible, but Maureen found solace in books.

When she read she escaped her wretched life. She lived in the stories she read. Her fantasy world was her reality. Maureen's mother, incidentally, was too terrified to do anything to help her. Eventually, I think, her father died and her life started to improve. The point I'm trying to make here is that Maureen survived her brutal childhood with the help of books. Maureen went on to become a children's author. In her case books were her saviour. No doubt there are scars. Deep scars. Maureen married but didn't want children. And, she even admitted to 'pretending life'. By that she meant she didn't want to look at what she was thinking or feeling, too much. It was all too painful; so she chose to 'pretend' to live. Maureen created a persona which she used as a mask. It was her way of coping and living some sort of life. In her words, she'd survived.

Most of us will have something in life that we have to deal with. For some of us it's sexual abuse. How we deal with it is determined by an assortment of variables: gender, generation, culture, family, upbringing/conditioning, social position, education, place in family, intelligence, etc. — it is a long list. So it is difficult to say that what affects one person is definitely going to affect another. There are similarities and some characteristics are shared in most cases. It is not safe to generalise too much. But features like low self-esteem and a derailed attitude to sex tend to be the most common shared elements.

Pick Up the Pieces

CHAPTER 12

Mind Your Language!

'Every word we say to children has the power to affect them'.

A most sobering thought. Scary but true. If ever there was a statement that could act as a contraceptive, this is it. Hearing the child psychologist say this on the radio stopped me in my tracks. It's obvious. How can it not be the case? Every time we open our mouths we want to have an effect, otherwise why would we bother saying anything at all. In fact we cannot even have a thought without first employing words. How can we *think* without *words*? We cannot influence our feelings, beliefs, thoughts or behaviour without using words first. So the language we use is very important.

But how can we be sure, particularly when talking to children, that we're having the effect that we intend to have? How do we know how it's being interpreted? Added to this is the *way* in which we say things: tone of voice, emphasis, volume, inflection. Mix in body-language, facial expression, gesticulation and eye-contact; getting a message across, then, can be fraught with problems. In fact it is a minefield. A sentence can have several different meanings when said in several different ways. For instance, a friend told me that her dad, gravely ill in hospital, turned his feeble head and whispered to her, '*Yours* is the last face I want to see before I die'. She was very fond of her father and he of her, so we can take it he meant that her face was the last thing he wanted to look upon before he died. Change the emphasis to 'Yours is the *last* face I want to see before I die' and it means totally the opposite.

So there are nuances we must be aware of before we open our mouths. Especially with children. Children are unable to filter or interpret the words we say to them in the way we want them to. To put it bluntly—they don't know what the hell we're on about a lot of the time. Children do not have knowledge or experience to decipher what we're saying because they haven't been around long enough—and they don't have a wide vocabulary as yet. However, in gaining this experience as they grow, they are likely to misinterpret some of our words along the way. Turning them into negatives sometimes.

Hence by the time they reach adulthood their hard-drive might contain a lot of unintended negative language which they then use against themselves. For example, 'Why don't you study hard like your sister?' when heard many times can be absorbed over the years as 'I can't study as well as my sister. I'm not as clever as my sister. I'm not very bright'. The comment may not have been meant to be negative but is worded clumsily and is left open to misinterpretation. It is important, therefore, to be as accurate as we can when talking to children.

Our self-deprecating culture and pseudo-modesty doesn't help to uphold positivity. Compliments are not something we accept with grace. We are often embarrassed when someone says something nice about us and we immediately play it down under the guise of modesty. Criticism, on the other hand, we welcome as truthful honesty—after all *there is no smoke without fire*.

Adele Faber's work with Elaine Mazlish on how to talk to children and how to listen so that they will talk shows how negative language impacts on them and the knock-on effects.[1] Their series of books on the same theme demonstrates how positives can turn this around. These experts show us how to respect children—treat them as human beings. Sometimes I think that because children are small in stature we view them as less than us adults—it's as if they can only gain respect by the kilo. And we deal with them as though they're the enemy: to be conquered and brought to submission. Faber and Mazlish:

---

1. *How to Talk So Kids Can Learn,* Adele Faber and Elaine Mazlish, Piccadilly Press, 2014. The various short quotes in this chapter appear in this work.

'If we value our children's dignity, then we need to model the methods that affirm their dignity. And we can't do that unless we show respect for what it is they're feeling.'

'Along with our words of respect we need *an attitude of respect*'.

Childhood should be a time when we're introduced to the world and prepared to deal with what life has to throw at us as we become adults. Instead, for many of us, we've spent a lot of our adulthood trying to make sense of what happened to us in childhood. But, as someone in the Hemel group discovered, it is never too late to have a happy childhood.

As adults/parents much of our child-rearing is about seeking to control children — make them malleable. To achieve this we have to undermine children's perception/interpretation of their feelings and experiences. As Faber and Mazlish say, our message to children is, 'You're wrong to feel what you feel. Listen to me instead.' In terms of sexual abuse, this is a catastrophic message.

Instead of feeding and growing self-confidence in children, we diminish it. Children need to hear unqualified acceptance of their emotions. Childhood should be about confidence-building, helping a child to trust its own feelings, allowing it to make mistakes and learn from them. Children need to feel we're on their side. When they feel attacked or not understood, children, like adults, become defensive. Our reaction then is to turn-up our power leading to a hollow victory for us and providing the child with further evidence that she/he is insignificant, unimportant, powerless and wrong.

I witnessed a good example of how to undermine a child's perception when I visited a friend. Her daughter and six-year-old granddaughter, Amy, were staying with her when Amy took a tumble down the stairs. No-one made a big deal of it. No-one rushed to comfort her. Yes, they did give her a mini-hug but followed it up with, 'Ah come on now, everything's fine. Stop fussing'. I was shocked at what I was witnessing. The little girl bawled real tears and was distraught. She showed them her little finger saying it was really, really sore. Then my friend turned to me and said, with Amy sitting on her lap, 'Ah she's always like this. Bit of a drama queen. A bit of a cry-baby, aren't you Amy? And look, there's nothing wrong with your finger at all?' My friend looked to me to back her up. I couldn't. I sat there dumbfounded.

Probably, Amy had earned her reputation of being a 'bit of a cry baby' because she'd not been believed in the past and was now in the process of accelerating the effect of an injury in an attempt to find out at what point she was actually going to be heard and believed. (Again, here is a child being treated as a liar).

A child's feelings are always in proportion to their age and experience. Whilst a bruised finger can be a huge issue to a child, to an adult it is not very much — which is why we play down their perception. More than likely, in the early days, Amy's family sought to quieten her down rather than calm her down.

Her finger was not damaged in the fall; it probably didn't hurt that much, but I think she needed to focus on something — anything — to get their attention — to be heard. I would have thought tumbling down a flight of stairs would have been enough. It certainly freaked me out to hear the bumpity-bump noise of her soft little body hitting the stairs and wall on her way down — so it must have at least shaken her up. No obvious scars didn't mean she didn't warrant a proper comforting hug and confirmation that falling down the stairs is a scary experience. It should have been acknowledged thus affirming that her feelings were real — and important.

As Faber and Mazlish suggest, we should, 'acknowledge the child's distress'. Yet time-and-time-again we block children's access to their own feelings for fear that they'll turn into hypochondriacs or neurotics. We fear them becoming out of our control. Our underlying message to them is, 'You're wrong to feel what you feel. Listen to me the adult, instead'. By continually deferring to adults a child will never learn how to trust its own feelings.

In place of self-trust there is adult-trust (and we all know where that can lead). How on earth is that preparing a child for life? Faber and Mazlish:

'If we value our children's dignity, then we need to model the methods that affirm their dignity. If we want to send out into the world young people who respect themselves and respect others then we need to begin by respecting them. And we can't do that unless we show respect for what it is they feel.'

We need to take children's worries seriously even though they may seem trivial to us. Not taking them seriously belittles the problem and belittles the child. And affirmation does not have to take the form of elaborate, effusive, smothering affirmation: 'Oh my poor darling little babykins that must have been soo bad,' etc. Sometimes just a gentle 'Hmm' in a soft tone of voice can be enough. It is the acknowledgement that counts. Showing acceptance of a child's perspective.

I know that I too was on the fast-track to becoming known as a neurotic, super-sensitive child. A crash into someone's garden fence whilst travelling in my father's sidecar proved it. 'Come on now, stop being hysterical,' I was told after being extracted from the wreckage. 'No-one's hurt. Stop panicking. It was just a little bump. Calm down for goodness sake, you're getting in such a state'. I was six-years-old. Of course I would be hysterical. Of course I'd be panicking. I remember not knowing what to do with my emotions. They were gushing out all over the place and I didn't know *how* to calm down — what did I actually have to *do*? I still don't know what it means. It's not a valid instruction. 'Take a nice, slow, deep breath and relax your muscles' is an instruction. I just needed someone to acknowledge that this was pretty scary for me — especially as I'd been dozing off when it happened and was therefore violently awoken by the impact.

Children need to hear unqualified acceptance of their emotions. They don't need our opinions — our evaluative comments — every time. They need to form their own opinions. Often we are inclined to grade what a child tells us. 'That doesn't hurt. It's only a little scratch' or 'That's not so bad. It'll heal'. Saying 'That's not so bad' tells the child that as an adult only we know how bad it is. You as a child don't. And we can undermine the child's perception of its experience and replace it with our own. How can that be right? Of course a child might 'over-react' in our eyes but it is trying to find its own reality and connect with its own feelings. In doing so it is going to get things 'wrong' or more accurately, out of proportion — but that is what childhood is about: finding our way, honing our understanding and making our own mistakes.

A child contained and restricted by an adult's perception of the world is vulnerable as the child is then unfamiliar with her or his own feelings and therefore unable to gauge situations safely for itself. A parent isn't with a child 24/7 so we have to prepare and help a child to rely on its own judgement and hope that they will make choices that keep them safe. However, that does not mean filling them with fear either, but age-related empowerment.

We learn primarily through repetition and our mistakes. If we're not allowed to learn life's lessons this way as children we are vulnerable. As parents, we seem to be terrified of a child 'getting things wrong' so we are inclined to prepare them for the worst — to warn them of all the dangers they might encounter in life. However, by telling a child of the dangers they will become more reluctant to experiment or discover the world for themselves. Even saying, 'Be careful' can have the effect of undermining a child as it could be interpreted as, 'They don't believe I can be careful because they have to *tell* me to be careful'. Talking is dangerous! And we probably do too much of it.

Also, nowadays we tend to view children as valuable possessions rather than valued individuals. They must be protected at all costs. This is admirable — but then we fail them spectacularly when it comes to protecting them from sexual abuse. In our conditioning of children we fail to give them a language (particularly about sex), and confidence in their ability to trust their own feelings; we bully them into being obedient; we frighten them into respecting all adults; we insist that politeness is paramount and punish them when they react with frustration. And then we wonder why they don't tell when they're abused.

If we follow this through we can see how language impacts on the issue of sexual abuse — especially in terms of protecting children and potentially reducing the prevalence of sexual abuse. I believe there are definite links between the language we use with children and the level of safety we can provide for them.

Accurate language = better understanding = improved awareness = increased confidence = a safer child.

This sounds like an over-ambitious, fantastical and downright dangerous statement to make. Indeed I've already been told by one rape crisis worker that the responsibility should remain fixed on the abuser and that focusing on the child makes abuse the child's fault. That is a complete misunderstanding and narrow view of what I'm saying. Of course sexual abuse is entirely the fault of the abuser alone. I'm not challenging that fact at all. As someone who was abused in childhood, I know only too well that it wasn't anything I did. But we're missing something here by solely holding on to that view. It needs expanding.

We know, for example, that if we don't lock our doors we could be burgled. With that knowledge we lock our doors and make them as secure as we can. We listen to and understand how burglars operate—in order to improve our knowledge and thus increase our safety. In the same way then with sex abuse, if we had better knowledge of how offenders abuse we could improve our children's safety. As I have already surmised in *Chapter 8* in relation to my own children, providing them with appropriate language to identify when they're feeling uncomfortable and bringing them up to be confident in their ability to listen to their feelings is important. Language is one of their tools; confidence is another.

I believe that had I had a healthy level of self-confidence and a language to talk about sexual matters, there would have been an increased chance that I would have been able to tell someone what had been happening; instead of remaining silent for 20-odd years.

But language is a tool not a weapon. And in giving children the appropriate tool of language we are not lulling them into a false sense of security.

I also know that even having an abundance of self-confidence is no assurance against abuse. There is no fail-safe way of protecting our children. As Robert Black said (in his interviews with Ray described in *Chapter 9*), 'You would have to tie your children to you 24/7 if you want to keep them totally safe from paedophiles'. But, because we cannot do that, at least we can look at/make ourselves aware of better methods of bringing them up. We as parents have a responsibility for their safety in every respect; and it is my belief that we can't ignore the fact that the way in which we bring-up our children risks robbing them of their right to autonomy. I believe that some aspects of our child-rearing methods actually help mould our children into perfect potential victims.

We like our children to be obedient, polite, to respect all adults, especially family members, we don't provide them with an adequate language about sex and we expect our children to trust us and not question our authority. The parents of one of Black's victims were baffled as to why this should have happened to their child because they'd brought her up the 'right way to be obedient, well behaved, polite and kind to other people'. Obviously, though none of these things could have determined her fate, it does show how much we value these qualities.

'Do as I say'.

'Why?

'Because I say so'.

This still holds as an axiom.

We boss children—for 'their own good'.

In bringing-up our children we will also be drawing on our own experiences from childhood. We will use much of what we learned from our own parents. The adage, 'Well, it never did me any harm' is often used to justify corporal punishment; it is a useful cliché some parents may resort to when things become overwhelming. A 'spoilt brat' melting-down in a packed restaurant would probably evoke the sympathy of other customers who see poor parents struggling to regain control. They might even be glad the child has been given a clip around the ear as it demonstrates the parents are capable of disciplining their child and also shows the parents' concern for other diners. Instead of reacting with embarrassment and hostility towards the child and asking it to 'behave nicely and stop lashing-out', an alternative approach might be, 'If you're angry, tell me in another way and I'll be glad to listen'. Or 'Use words not fists to tell me how you feel'.

Each time we show a child that we accept what they're saying they will be one step forward in being able to trust their own feelings. Of course we may not always agree with them but children, like adults, need that feeling of being heard. It is affirming and creates an opportunity for discussion rather than argument. The word 'uncomfortable' is important. Most children recognise the difference between feeling *comfortable* and *uncomfortable*. By teaching a child to tune into the word *uncomfortable* we are providing them with the tool to do a 'sense-check'. In other words if a child feels doubtful in any situation then asking her/him to ask, 'Do I feel comfortable with this?' is a good start. My daughter uses it with her children. She introduced it a while ago but not in the context of a *birds and bees* type talk. Her method weaves it into the fabric of her children's childhood — like teaching them to cross the road.

I'm not saying that as a parent I got it right all the time with my children. Not even some of the time. When I look back I can see chasms in their childhoods where I got things badly wrong. I know there were many occasions where I didn't listen and did resort to 'traditional' methods. But I got a couple of things right — enough to have helped keep them safe when they were in danger — that and luck. Hopefully, they had enough of a positive upbringing which contributed to the confident people they are today. If I knew then what I know now their childhoods would have been far, far better.

Realising the things I could have said and done differently when they were young is difficult for me. But it's never too late to start trying. In terms of evaluative and graded comments, I am certainly guilty. Praise is not necessarily a positive thing as we might think it to be. In grading a child — i.e. 'You're brilliant', we are setting that child up to fail. 'Well if I'm brilliant, I don't have to try any more' or 'How can I stay being brilliant, what will happen if I become unbrilliant?'

So, using my newly-acquired knowledge from the work of Faber and Mazlish mentioned earlier in this chapter, I thought I'd employ a non-evaluative approach with one of my students. I'd been doing some home-tutoring and had had great trouble reading Sean's handwriting. Sean was nine-years-old. His parents were exasperated with him as were his teachers. No-one could read a thing he'd written. And I was no exception.

Sean's writing resembled a drunken spider doing the tango across the page. His parents were expecting me to scold him and harangue him into writing properly. They wanted me to adopt their approach — but

I knew it wouldn't work. Scolding, accusing and withholding privileges only served to exacerbate an already difficult situation. Sean could no longer hear what the adults were saying and he was angry because he was always in the wrong.

I began, 'Sean, when you leave spaces between the words, they become clearer'.

The following week there were gigantic spaces separating the words. Too wide, but never mind, he'd listened and taken it on board.

A couple of weeks later, 'Sean when your letters sit on the line your writing is easier to read'.

Hey presto words stood to attention on the line.

Another few sessions later, 'Sean, you could get more words on the line if the letters were smaller'.

I was on a roll. His progress was cumulative. When he got it right, rather than praise him with 'You're brilliant', etc., I commented on the improved writing, drawing attention to its new legibility.

'Sean why do you think your writing goes straight through to the second and third page?'

'I press too hard?'

'How could that be prevented from happening?'

'I won't press too hard?'

Yes! Result. Sean had worked it all out for himself. The next week he couldn't wait to tell me that his teacher had said he could now start using a proper pen. After a while, Sean's handwriting evolved into a beautiful script. All I'd done was comment on the facts. No flattery, threats, chastisements or impatience. I gave him space to come to his own conclusions. Though, I have to admit I so wanted him to tell me how good a tutor I'd been in helping him improve his writing. The drunken spider was now sober and waltzing elegantly across the page.

Even in his interviews with Black, Ray insisted on using accurate language. It was vital. So, where Black would refer to a child's vagina as a 'fanny', Ray would correct him. This was important because, by applying a colloquial or slang term to any aspect of sexual abuse, the abuser minimises his offence. He attempts to diminish his behaviour and its impact.

Faber and Mazlish point out that 'Punishment teaches a child to lie, to feel hostile, angry, vengeful. They learn that it's okay for the adult to mete out punishment but that they must not... until they become the one in charge'. A child who has been bullied will more than likely become a bully. We're all aware of that adage. As I've mentioned before the majority of offenders in treatment claim to have been abused themselves. Certainly that they, having been abused, became the abusers is learned behaviour.

Punishment may not always take the form of hitting. Sarcasm, humiliation, shouting, rejection, mocking, scolding, being rude — when we employ these methods all we are doing is showing children *how* it's done. We are giving them, through example, the weapons to use in later life. Punishment begets cruelty. Even 'time-out' can be harmful. 'Forced isolation is often humiliating for a child. It creates anger and a feeling of rejection' according to Faber and Mazlish. The message is 'I don't want to be with you when you need me the most'.

This new way of relating to children is all very well but in a crisis for sure it could all go out of the window. Who can tell Daniel, in a live situation, that kicking seven bells out of little Mikey isn't allowed — and that it's better to *tell* Mikey what you don't like, with words rather than your boots. Being in a volatile situation is not the time to start learning. As Faber and Mazlish agree — when someone is drowning it is not the time to teach them to swim! That is why we have to read and re-read books like theirs. Outside of a crisis situation we have to practice and practice it until it becomes second nature. Then, in a crisis situation it has a better chance of being a useful and valuable tool.

Behavioural Insights

In 2017, the Behavioural Insights Team (BIT) (a partly government-resourced body established in 2010) published a practical guide for parents, teachers and school leaders addressing the issue of conditioning children. BIT is interested in applying more realistic models of human behaviour with the objective of helping people make better decisions for themselves. It believes in developing a child's ability to 'understand their current knowledge, to be comfortable with questioning both [itself] and others to seek answers, to pick themselves up after setbacks and to persevere through times of uncertainty'.[2] BIT wants to promote meta-cognition i.e. the ability to understand one's own thinking processes.

All these ideas are language-dependent. Even the way we phrase a question will have an impact on the response. Wording a response in a certain way can either open up the subject for further discussion or close it down. BIT gives an example:

> 'Tom wants to tell his mother how he learned about the solar system at school and lists several new facts he has learned. Tom's mother could, instead of closing the subject with an enthusiastic, "That's brilliant!", might encourage the thought process further with, "That's brilliant; what other planets are there? Do they have moons too?" This invites Tom to explore what he has learned and develop his thoughts. Therefore, parents can use everyday conversations to develop their child's metacognitive skills just by asking questions that inspire curiosity'.

This in turn improves and hones their child's confidence in his or her own findings thus contributing to the child's ability to trust its own feelings. And obviously language plays a vital role in this. After all, in order to change any behaviour, beliefs, thinking or feelings we must employ *words*. We cannot have a single thought without using them. Our own internal monologues, be they positive or negative, are, quite simply, *words*. BIT goes much further in exploring and explaining these methods and their practical guide is a highly recommended read.

Other Work on Positive Conditioning

Also, hot on the trail of positive conditioning in childhood is Suzanne Zeedyk,[3] a research scientist based at Dundee University. Her work centres/focuses on exploring/investigating babies/children's capacity to connect with us. She focuses on how our treatment of babies impacts

---

2. See www.behaviouralinsights.co.uk
3. See www.suzannezeedyk.com

and shapes them as people. Emotional trauma in childhood doesn't end when that traumatic episode/experience stops. Emotions, Zeedyk tells us, live in our bodies and do not simply dissipate when we grow. They can stay with us into adulthood and affect every area of our lives. An extreme emotional experience literally sends messages to the growing brain and impedes its natural development causing neurological impairments that can result in health problems in adult life. Apply this theory to sexual abuse and it is no surprise that there is a high proportion of self-harm, depression, alcoholism, etc. Tragically, the list of potentially adverse consequences is virtually endless.

When a traumatic event obstructs the way our brains are naturally evolving, that obstruction remains. Growth then finds a different path– different from the route it was intending to take. A young brain moulds and adapts to the reality it faces and lives in.

No-one, I think, would disagree with Zeedyk's philosophy that, 'The decisions we take about caring for our children are integrally connected to our vision for the kind of society we wish to build'.

She also advocates means of communication other than language such as laughing, hugging, listening, breathing (slowly, deeply) all of which are effective ways of reassuring and connecting and communicating with a child. Language does, however, play an important role in supporting and implementing all these theories.

When Methods Fail

So, what if all the improved language and confidence-building methods fail? What happens when, in spite of what we've learned and passed on to our children, a child is sexually abused? How do we pick-up the pieces then?

I don't think a child imbued with sound knowledge, a healthy self-confidence and an ability to trust its own feelings, etc. will fare the same as a child who has not been brought up in the same way. This is because the child is more likely to feel it could talk to someone; she or he is likely to have an inner rescuing language that doesn't apportion blame to herself/himself and it lessens the destructive element of secrecy. She or he will have those important tools that will help them limit the damage that could impact on them. They will survive better. I'm trying desperately not to generalise or be prescriptive here—what I'm saying is that I believe in increasing chances of safety in any way. Language is one way.

Horrible stuff happens in life but then we are each the sum total of our life's experience. And even now, I'm about to grade my own experience of sexual abuse in order to 'qualify' for the next statement: My experience of childhood abuse rates about medium to high on the Richter scale of abuse. It's probably in the orange zone. And yes, I did have rescuing hands that kept me from descending totally into the pit. I know I was lucky. But I believe that, in a high majority of rubbish childhoods, there is a way of curtailing the damage. There is a way unique to each of us to survive. *Accepting* that because of a childhood experience we may not have turned out as we might have done can be better than *battling* with the effects.

For example, being involved in a car crash as a child might result in a permanent limp. Pretending that that limp isn't there, or not recalling the crash, may not necessarily mean that all is healed. Denial doesn't always work. Rather it can create a cumulative situation that can turn into a time-bomb. Maybe an acceptance that the crash happened will enable that experience to inform future decisions, e.g. it may make that child a more cautious driver later. It may result in that child taking a medical interest in his/her condition. In my own case, being an abused child helped me help others. Though I have to say, I wouldn't recommend it as a way of understanding how an abused person feels. In some respects my childhood was shattered, but I'd like to think I have picked-up the pieces and that my grandfather's abuse didn't result in what he intended for me. Quite the opposite in fact—and he didn't get away with it because now I've told the world—well anyone who reads this book—about what he did. No more secrets.

I believe we are born with our instincts to trust our own feelings intact. Childhood, instead of pairing these instincts to experience and knowledge so that they grow and work in harmony, now takes us away from our instincts and instead substitutes an intellectually-informed radar in their place. By that I mean, instead of allowing our feelings (instincts) to influence decision-making we rely too much on intellectual information/conditioning. We have moved too far away from the instinct-informed way of being that we were born with. Consequently we have developed a hunger for books that might lead us back to a more instinctual way of decision-making. Hence the massive success of self-help books. It cannot be denied that there is an increasing dependency on self-help manuals which set out to reconnect us to our inner-selves. We are having to relearn how to trust ourselves and our instincts. Learning (or relearning) how to achieve this retrospectively isn't as effective as absorbing it into our hard-drive/blueprint as a child. It is a more cerebral experience than a honed naturally-evolving instinct but it's better than nothing and it is ironic that we turn to even more cerebral feeding (i.e. books) to achieve it.

Relying almost solely on logic, intellect and what we've been told as a coping mechanism can be dangerous. The example of my daughter and I being followed around the market by the man from Houghton Regis (*Chapter 4*) is one. *Logic* could have told me that he just happened to be going my way and just happened to be behind us on the same route. *Instinct* told me this was not right because I felt uncomfortable. I trusted my feelings. His odd response when questioned by the policeman confirmed my instinct was right—he had indeed been following us.

Though the man in the lift experience (again see *Chapter 4*) was almost entirely due to the melded voices in my head telling me it was okay to get into the lift with him, those voices did hold a level of logic. Why wouldn't anyone get into a lift with a stranger? After all, people do it all the time and nothing happens to them. It was a logic that won and placed me in a dangerous situation.

The example of my son, Adam, on feeling uncomfortable with the man whose car he and his friend Michael were washing (same chapter), also shows that if he'd responded with logic there would have been a different outcome. Logically, RD hadn't actually done anything other than chat to the boys, invite them in for an orange juice, and give them ten pounds from which they had to return with the change. Nothing *logically* wrong with any of that. But Adam allowed himself to trust his instinct and told us of his feelings of uncomfortableness. For sure Michael was operating from logic and intellect because he'd said nothing to his parents at all about the encounter. Because there was no actual evidence that this man had ulterior motives, Michael had nothing to report.

I am not claiming that instinct over intellect always gets it right. No. Mixing the two increases the chances of getting it right. The more we employ instincts peppered with intellect our chances of improving safety will be increased. In other words allowing ourselves to trust our own feelings will improve the way we make choices. We prioritise better.

Using 'accurate' language with children is, and can be, effective in building confidence. A confident child is better placed when assessing situations which may lead to danger—as Adam's experience shows. No doubt there will be those who will read this and challenge my thinking—but discussion is what is needed.

Familiarity

Familiarity plays a significant part in impeding the transition from trusting logic to trusting instinct. Usually when we seek counselling it is because our old well-honed coping strategies are no longer effective as we once believed them to be. These old strategies are likely to contain misinterpreted messages from childhood, negative language, intellectually-informed choices resulting in a disconnection from instinct, feeling lost and a sense of not knowing who we are.

In counselling we may start seeing things differently—we begin to learn a new way of thinking and being and see ourselves more positively. A good counsellor will help us focus on the facts and reality of who we are instead of allowing untrue negatives about ourselves to remain in power. Counselling, though sometimes difficult and sometimes traumatic, can deliver us to a new, positive place. And hence we move forward often enjoying the 'new me'. However, new me is *new*—and therefore unfamiliar. And this unfamiliarity can feel scary and alien: it is unknown territory. As the counselling process isn't a straight continuous road, there are times when we will go back to the old ways of thinking and being, not necessarily because we want to but because it's a familiar place. Even though we know it didn't work and doesn't work anymore.

This is not regression as many people may experience it. We do not stay back in the old-way permanently but, because we've already tried the 'new way' of thinking, feeling and being, we come back to it. We return to that point where we learned the truth about ourselves and better ways of being. So then we travel a little further into the 'new way' — discover a bit more. Then, again we might go back to the old way because of the power of its familiarity. But that is okay, as each time we make this journey from new to old and back to new, the path itself becomes familiar and will eventually start to feel safe. The old way only acts to undermine the new way and assert its seniority simply because it's been around ever since we can remember. Positive affirmation is like rehearsing a script. The more times we say it the better chance it has of sticking. Through repetitive positive affirmation we, in a sense, brain-wash ourselves with the truth.

There are a variety of triggers that can snap us back to the old way of thinking and being. These can range from exhaustion, a hurtful comment made by someone, the practicalities of life or simply the unfamiliarity of the new way and we must 'forgive' ourselves when this happens.

In anything new that we try — whatever it may be — the draw of familiarity must never be underestimated. Familiarity, even when heinously destructive or dangerous, is so potent as to render people powerless to change their situations. Many, many people abused in childhood, or women in unbelievably violent relationships, remain in them because that is all they know — it is *familiar.* And within this familiarity there is a sense of 'safety' — it is a known place. *Better the devil you know* is what keeps us all from moving forward.

A colleague of mine, B, from many years ago, stayed in a dreadfully abusive relationship. Her husband would beat her, rape her, verbally abuse her, humiliate her in front of people. She went out to work whilst he lazed at home. B was terrified of him but wouldn't leave even though, when she left him each morning to go to work, we couldn't understand why she didn't run away. No matter how we tried to help, she stayed put. But, she explained, this life was all she knew and anyway if she behaved in the way he wanted she didn't always incur his wrath. So she held herself partly to blame. He told her she was fat — so she lost weight. He told her he didn't like long hair—so she cut it. Her cooking wasn't right—so she only cooked what he wanted. Not getting it right always meant a thrashing. B believed that, by acting a certain way, she had some control. Not true. She was tragically wrong. After another inhuman beating B eventually died from her internal injuries. He was tried for manslaughter.

Another aspect of accurate language has, for a long time, puzzled me and that is the subject of surrogacy. I've noted that when a woman 'donates an egg' to an infertile women it is called 'donating an *egg*'. However, a woman who cannot actually carry a baby may have her own (fertilised) egg implanted in another woman and claim the child as hers because it is *genetically* her child. The woman carrying that child then becomes the 'surrogate'. For sure I'm missing something here. Is it a case of changing the language to suit ourselves?

If not knowing our genetic origins is not important to us why are programmes such as *Who do You Think You Are?* and *Long Lost Family* so popular? Are we deliberately creating people who can never know their genetic parents purely to suit a particular situation—and are we hiding behind semantics?

Analysis of Black's Dialogue

The *Murder of Childhood* inspired me to write this book. In reading it I realised just how important and powerful language is and how much we rely on words for communication. It became clearer on re-reading *MoC* that, apart from the obvious message that we should be learning from sex-offenders in order to protect our children, we should also make ourselves language-aware. It is fair to say that language analysis played a key role in Ray's work. After all, it is language that influences behaviour. Observing Black's use of words in his interviews with Ray allows us to see (but not accept) how he distorted his thinking in order to believe that, for example, murdering a child victim would be better for her than 'allowing' her to suffer. Black's ability to convince himself is astounding and Ray clearly makes the connection between language and behaviour. I have included examples from one passage below.

Mind Your Language!

Words reveal more about us than maybe we would like. And, as with each and every one of Ray's clients, it is the words they used that gave them 'permission' to abuse or kill. As with Gracewell's client Eric and his grooming of Steven (*Chapter 10*), the words he chose to describe his so called 'one-off' offence, merely set out to diminish and excuse his abusive behaviour. They were not an attempt to accept responsibility at all. Steve was attempting to deceive his fellow offenders and failed spectacularly. Most, if not all, of Black's dialogue sets out to dilute his crimes and allow him to present himself as a victim who didn't understand his own self. Under closer analysis it becomes clearer what he is trying to do, as the following short extract demonstrates

> 'I don't know who made the approaches [I didn't initiate it; tries to show casualness]. I know [emphatic] it wasn't me [creates a distance] because I was called [suggesting he was invited] in afterwards [implying he was only a bystander—it was an afterthought] and it seemed [she gave me the impression; I didn't misinterpret it] she'd agreed [confirms what I want you to believe—that it was her idea not mine] for a cigarette, to let us have a look [implying that, again, it was her idea and that she was in control]. The girl dropped [a powerful verb suggesting immediacy and a keenness on her part] her knickers and she said "You want to have a look here?" [Black wants Ray to believe that it was she who had the power and he was merely going along with her request]. And I just [minimising] had a look [a disinterested glance] and I think [it was so insignificant] I touched her [admits to some less serious physical contact]…I don't know [again pretending it was so insignificant that he can't even remember]. And then she said, like [using meaningless "fillers"] she was the boss [wants Ray to believe it was she who had the position of power], she'd had enough [wants to convince Ray his victim had a choice]. When she'd had her fag, that was it'.

This last sentence denigrates the girl further — a fag is all she was worth because that is all she wanted. When she got that, it was all over. Also the word 'fag' is a diminution of 'cigarette' which he used earlier. So, the whole effect of these final sentences encapsulates his distorted beliefs: that he is not to blame, that the victim is the one who was really responsible and that he has no respect for and cannot relate to others.

Throughout his interviews with Ray, Black demonstrated his ability to use reductive, evasive language. Language he had clearly used all his life which he had honed, cultivated and that enabled him to carry out his heinous murders. In a sense the words he used gave him 'permission' to do what he did.

He claimed to believe that, by killing the child he was abusing, he was saving her from pain. How many times would he have had to say that to himself before he truly believed it? How could he ever justify and believe that murdering a child was in her best interests?

Ray's adherence to accurate language was strict. During the sessions he insisted that Black use correct terminology so he didn't elude from the reality of his acts. For instance an offender might refer to oral sex as a 'blow-job' when in actual fact he was describing a sex act he has forced his victim to perform. Ray: 'The use of plain words is important for the therapist too. The non-descriptive terms form a language that has meaning in quite a different context'.

Failure to correct an offender during treatment allows them to evade confronting the impact their abuse had on their victim(s). When Black says he 'just took a look' at the vagina of one of his victims and found her to be bruised, it begs the question: How on earth had she been bruised by him 'just looking'?

Pick Up the Pieces has sought to reiterate the message that language is powerful, not only in an interpersonal and everyday context but also to show why we should be looking at the way we speak to children.

Epilogue

I cannot fully understand my excessive feelings and attraction towards Ray other than his fatal charisma. As I've said before, he was a bit of a Marmite, really—you either loved him or you didn't. I, unfortunately, loved him to destruction. It was a reciprocal love that was hugely detrimental to both of us. I didn't want him to leave my side and I didn't want to leave his side. I loved him to bits. I wish I could tell him that right now. In turn he allowed the funny, playful side of me to thrive. We brought out the child in each other and had such fun at times. In fact a sense of humour became a valuable coping mechanism for me as time went on. A necessity even.

However, further down the road, his unacceptable domestic habits went beyond the pale. He needed a mother, skivvy, cook, saint, an amoeba. It went further than just being lazy. Way, way beyond. It would be unkind to list it all anyway. I'm sure there was a gremlin at work deep inside his psyche.

Together we created a time-bomb that was set to go off in 2007 when I couldn't take any more and asked for some time-out. He was devastated. I was devastated. We remained married until his death but lived separately though, even then, we were working on a plan for our future togetherness that we could both live with. I believe death was the only way we could be separated because we were too involved with one another. He said I'd got under his skin and he couldn't let go. He did truly love me. I have all the cards and letters and jewellery to keep that love safe and warm. And if I start to miss him too much I only have to recall the financial carnage he left me with after his death, to put things in perspective and not forgetting the relationships with his friends and family that cannot be rebuilt because of it.

That I am only now free of that mess is due to my own strength and tenacity. I survived and picked-up the pieces—again. The rollercoaster that lasted from 2008 to 2012 began on the 20th June 2008.

'Goodnight, Sweetheart'

The night before Ray died we'd gone out to dinner at Whittlebury Hall in Towcester. Ray usually had steak and chips or something else typically unsuitable for an overweight diabetic—accompanied with Diet Coke. It must be Diet Coke, is it *Diet* Coke? Yes, it's a Diet Coke—would be the usual conversation with waiting staff. Thursday, 19th June, however, was different—a portentous change from the usual fare. Ray had the fish. And he ordered a jug of sangria to wash it down with. No Diet Coke. All very un-Ray. Was this a last-ditch attempt to save himself? But it was a lovely romantic dinner seasoned with affectionate touches and glances. We were discussing a way of being together separately that suited both of us.

Back home, Ray sprawled on the sofa and I massaged his feet as I had done hundreds of times before. He was soon to be heading back to his little house/office which he now shared with his son, Tim. At about 9.40 pm Ray left, waving to me as he drove over the grass and budding petunias. I rolled my eyes then blew him a kiss. I would never see him alive again.

> Friday 20th June 2008 11 am: I am in Leicester working with a client Ray has referred to me. I've been here from 10 am having parked in the multi-storey and walked through the market. I'd seen a pair of jeans hanging-up on one of the stalls and swaying in the breeze and thought I'd check them out after the session. My client is a lovely lady. At 10.50 we take a break and she goes out for a smoke. My phone rings, Ray's number comes up. Before I have a chance to say, 'Hi darling', I hear Tim's voice.
>
> I immediately thought it's one of the dogs; he's let them out and one of them has been run over. 'Char, it's Tim. We've lost him, Char'. Oh my God it's Louie (one of our dogs) he's run-off and Ray's out looking for him;

but no. 'It's dad. He's gone, Char'. Tim's voice is miraculously calm and soothing as he stabs my heart with his words. More is said to clarify the brutal truth and I'm left here in this room, alone. The world is still here, I haven't heard a bomb go off. As I drift into the corridor a security guard is walking by and I tell him something about my husband but I can't get the last word out. He gets me some water and my client's social worker comes down to see me. She offers to take me to the station. I decline. Leaving my car here would just cause more problems. I put my notepad, pen and newspaper calmly into my case. I close it and I ask her to accompany me to the motorway as I cannot remember how to get there.

11.45 am: Walking back to the car park I pass the jeans still hanging-up in the market. They're not swaying but remain respectfully still. I don't want them now. My daughter phones as I'm still walking to my car. She's unaware of the earthquake. It's noisy here and my gentle, 'Ray has passed away' is not heard so I shout down the phone, 'Ray has died!' The truth of it shocks me as much as it shocks her. It ricochets around the shopping mall. People are staring at me.

I drop the social worker off at the motorway junction and know not how she got back. And I drive, oh so carefully, homeward. I am in shocked overdrive. It seems a very long journey and my destination is getting further the longer I drive. I'm trying not to think. The signs for Crick are still there. So is the scenery.

1.40 pm: I arrive. There is no-one at home. I realise that the dogs need letting out. My daughter arrives and I start to focus. My son arrives. Pete (my ex) arrives. This is my family. My support team has grouped. Lucy has cancelled her trip to Scotland and is staying put with me. Her fiancé, Gavin, leaves to go and catch the plane to Edinburgh where his parents live—but not before he transfers a 'buffer' to my bank account. It hadn't occurred to me that bills would still have to be paid.

3.30 pm: We go the mortuary. Only I go in. There he lies cold, still sporting that wry smile: The love of my life. I reflect on what we were doing 24 hours earlier—he annoying the dogs and having a Diet Coke. And now he has stopped living. I can't process this. It's comforting to be with him here on our own and to talk to him. To scold him that he's broken his promise. 'Why did you leave me?' For once he is not distracted. He's not even thinking about his next malevolent rapist. He's not thinking about anything. Ray is just lying there. Being dead. I thought he was invincible. He thought he was invincible. We were both wrong. 'Bye bye, my darling. Goodnight, Sweetheart'.

I visited him another three times before it became 'inadvisable to see him now', the funeral director told me.

Picking Up the Pieces

The following month went by in a haze. My daughter Lucy got married in Scotland on the 4th July, my graduation was on the 9th (I'd just completed my English Literature degree) and Ray's funeral took place on the 15th. During all this I was battling with the finances because suddenly everything had stopped. Nothing was coming in. My mum, bless her, had to pay for Ray's funeral because I had no money. I needed to hang on to Gavin's emergency fund for the mortgage repayments. Secrets crawled like maggots out of his bank statements and devastating revelations showed that Ray was pretty much bankrupt. Prior to our living separately he'd signed the house over to me on the proviso that the remortgage would include a massive payout to himself.

That meant a £318,000 mortgage solely in my name with him acting as an unsecured guarantor—and with no life assurance in place. It was an interest-only business mortgage and the repayments were £1,200 a month.

'Don't worry, I'll give you enough money to cover it every month'. He hadn't set-up a standing order to pay me this regularly. I had to hope he'd remember—or to remind him. And of course, there were no instructions for me as to how I would make payments in the event of his death. How the TSB could have granted an unsecured loan of that size to a relatively small business, and called it responsible banking, is beyond me. It speaks as much about them as it does about Ray's charismatic persuasive manner. I had come to this marriage with an extremely healthy bank balance that should've meant no mortgage at all. But he'd conjured it away within months of our getting together.

Repossession loomed. My counselling contract with his company obviously ceased and I had just one contract left as a means of income. Turning the house into a B&B didn't bring in enough money, though the TSB did allow me, in their benevolence, to pay the mortgage instalments in cash every month. So every, third of the month, I'd collect, borrow and scrape the money together and take it to the bank in a carrier bag. Everyone thought I was rolling in it. I was. But what I was rolling in didn't smell too good.

It was October 2008 and we were in the midst of the recession. With job cuts awash, my son-in-law, sadly, was made redundant. Unfortunately for me, though, his desire to return to his native Scotland was realised when, in spite of the recession, he landed a job with the NHS in Glasgow. This meant of course that my daughter, who was by now expecting my first grandchild, would be whisked away from me. I was heartbroken. A couple of months before my grandson's birth, they left.

Engulfed by all the emotion and desperation, I decided to sell up and follow them. The house would not realise its true value in the economic downturn, but worse, Ray had had Bob the Builder from the village do some structural work on the roof. When a survey was carried out, the work was deemed inadequate and would not meet planning regulations. The cost of putting it right was estimated at £35,000. Consequently, no building society would grant a mortgage on the property. It was unsellable.

Meanwhile, people who hadn't been paid by Ray for various assessment work were snapping at my heels. Thirty-thousand-pounds here, £90,000 there. Her Majesty's Revenue and Customs was bearing down and so were all the credit card companies. My persecution complex flourished. It seemed everyone was gunning for me. I became defensive and unpleasant to deal with; I even began to believe someone had put a curse on me. In desperation I visited a Tarot card reader. She confirmed that 'someone was determined to get me'. As to whom that might be, I was spoilt for choice.

The house finally sold for just about the outstanding mortgage figure, to an angel of a lady who bought it for cash. So, off to Scotland I scampered believing I was now leaving all my worries behind and entering a new and better phase of my life. Alas, I couldn't have been more wrong. It was during this time that I discovered there was another layer to the bottom of the pit.

There were times when I felt truly suicidal — or more accurately that I began to question the point of living. Looking over the abyss was actually reassuring and even empowering: I didn't have to live this life if I didn't want to. No one could make me stay. I *did* have a choice. And it was the belief that I had a choice that kept me alive.

When you're feeling so desperate and pointless, believing that you still have to stick with it, is not a rescuing thought. I think it pushes you further towards the edge. Guilt-trips do not work. Thoughts about the children, the grandchildren, or the dogs do not pull you back from the brink — if anything, they push you further towards it because you believe everyone would be better off without you. Keeping a stiff upper lip is just denial. Crying (and I've done too much of that) exhausts you and affirms your helplessness. Staring at a gin bottle and a handful of tablets, however, gives you a choice — it helps you feel you have control of this mess — that you have got contingency plans in place.

Besides, this place was familiar to me. Hadn't I been here before — looking at a bottle of pills and contemplating a way out? At the age of 14 I often fondled a bottle of blue 10 mg pills belonging to my asthmatic younger brother. Ephedrine I think they were. It was always reassuring to know where they were — to feel 'safe'.

Work was non-existent in Scotland; the weather was depressing and I felt so terribly lonely without all that was familiar to me. I couldn't keep leaning on my daughter — she had her life to lead and I hadn't come up here to be a burden. I'd come to help and be part of my grandson's life. I kept the depth of my feelings to myself. Around this time I also lost my last telephone-support contract and last means of income.

I took a job as a cleaner with the NHS and also started conducting funeral services (it seemed fitting) as a means of earning a living. But in the end I felt the best thing to do was to pack up and come back home.

Epilogue

So, I returned to Milton Keynes to pick up where I left off in my journey to me.

How Am I Doing Nowadays?

Even with my darling dogs Penny and Louie now gone and ill-health beckoning, I find I am content with my lot. My children are happily married to people I respect. Anika, my son's wife joined the family in 2013. Today I have four of the most beautiful grandchildren anyone could wish for and a wonderful support network of dear friends. I picked-up the best pieces and built a nice life for myself.

I hope that we as a society will see the importance of working with sex-offenders and give freedom and support to those brave enough to do the work. We owe them much. We owe it to our children.

If I have any advice to pass on, it is this—in bringing up children it might be good to:

- **Ignore a lot:** If I had just ignored the selfish parking by former neighbours instead of complaining then maybe my tyres wouldn't have been let down. And they moved away not long after anyway.
- **Say little:** I'm glad I kept my mouth shut about a colleague's husband who I saw regularly going into a woman's house down the road. Had I said anything I would have forfeited the invitation to her 40th birthday party where her husband surprised her by singing *Unchained Melody*. The mysterious visits had been for singing lessons. Oops!
- **Be aware of everything:** I'm so glad I kept myself aware of Lucy's odd little lapses of concentration without panicking and making a big issue of it. Instead alerting doctors to her behaviour. When she had her *grand mal* she was already at the top of the list for epileptic diagnosis and treatment. Had I ignored the mini-lapses (*petit mals*) without seeking help and advice, by the time she had the major one she would only have been

on the first rung of the ladder with many *grand mals* ahead before she received effective treatment.

I mean that we might be better off *ignoring a lot* of the useless stuff we tend to pounce on children for. I gave up telling Lucy to tidy her room — it was pointless. Her half-hearted job just incensed me more. So I stopped bothering about it. I thought her adult home would be a shambles. I was so wrong. She has grown into a tidy person and her home is spick and span! I can't believe it.

Listening to Lucy and Adam arguing and arguing in the back of the car when they were children invited me to shout at them to stop. But that was futile. The less I said to them the more they shut up. I just tuned-out and let them get on with it. I learned that *saying little* has its place.

But I did try to make myself *aware of everything*. This meant observing and processing the subtle messages children leak when all is not okay. It meant being aware of everything because being aware *is* everything.

I hope that we begin to look at how we speak to children and that we learn to respect them without fearing them. It's never too late to learn new ideas along the way. Though some of us may feel we've got more wrong than we've got right, all is never lost. I've learned that children are resilient and more accepting as they grow into adults. As the song goes, *Children Are Our Future*.

What I would like to see for the future is an increased awareness of how we treat children. Discussion at the school gate — or anywhere for that matter — where debate, exchanges of opinions can take place by parents, grandparents, anyone involved with children and even those who are not. I just want people to start talking about child-protection and looking at how our own childhoods have affected us as adults. Talking and sharing ideas, experiences — and ways forward. We simply cannot ignore the issue of abusers and how our ignorance protects them. We need to talk.

Recommended reading

Forward, Susan (2nd revised edn. with Craig Buck), 2002, *Toxic Parents: Overcoming Their Hurtful Legacy and Reclaiming Your Life*, Bantam Books.

Jeffers, Susan, 2017 (revised edn.), *Feel the Fear and Do It Anyway*, Ebury.

Norwood, Robin, 2004 (new edn.), *Women Who Love Too Much*, Arrow.

Tannen, Deborah, 1990, *You Just Don't Understand: Women and Men in Conversation*, Ballantine Books.

Wyre, Ray, Tate, Tim and Richardson, Charmaine, *The Murder of Childhood: Inside the Mind of One of Britain's Most Notorious Child Murderers*, 2018 (2nd edn.), Waterside Press.

Index

abduction *83*
abuse *56, 59, 80*
   abusers *85, 87*
   child sexual abuse *vii*
   scale of abuse *122*
Adam *71, 123*
affection *79*
affirmation *113, 125, 134*
Aggie Weston's *52*
air raid shelter *66, 80*
Albany Prison *52*
alcohol *104*
Alice *56*
alienation *86, 102*
alternative to criminal process *17*
altruism *99*
ambition *43*
anger *45, 85, 95, 104*
   public anger *76*
apologies *95*
Asplands Medical Health Centre *56*
Australia *61*
autonomy *vi, 44, 116*
behavioural insights *119*
Belfast *51*
belonging *46*
bigotry *14, 64, 76*
Birmingham *13, 17, 68, 90*
   Birmingham Bible College *52*

blackmail *29*
Black, Robert *14, 65*
   adoption *78*
   Black's history *78*
   interviews with *75*
blame *17, 33, 40, 104*
borstal *82*
Bramshill *56*
bravado *58*
bullying *37, 106, 114, 119*
Bury Mill Family Centre *13*
Cardy, Jennifer *77*
castration *18*
Catholicism *26, 31*
Certificate in Social Work *52*
Chatterbox *37*
children *21*
Christopher (brother) *21*
Clark, Hector *84*
comfort-eating *104*
complicity *34*
conditioning *107, 119, 123*
   positive conditioning *120*
conferences *62, 76*
confidence *57, 62*
control *49, 60, 75, 98, 102, 104, 126*
coping *107, 123, 129*
Coral *45*
counselling *13, 46, 53, 124*

Crown Prosecution Service 72
cruelty 79, 119
crusade 67
curiosity 120
damage 35
danger 81
daydreaming 28
degradation 104
de-humanising 86
denial 17, 84, 122
dependency 61
depression 43, 105
dignity 111, 113
dirty
    feeling dirty 28
distortion 65, 77, 81, 94
distraction 77, 106
distress 112
DNA 97
doubt 38
drug-taking 105
Dunstable 40
Ealing 30
eating disorders 63, 104
embarrassment 17, 103
emotions 58, 60, 85, 121
empathy 58, 85
empowerment 55, 72, 84, 104
    children of 114
enthusiasm 18
Eric 91
evasion 17, 84
    evasive language 128
eye-contact 27, 57, 109
Faber, Adele 110

façade 45
familiarity 124
family 21
fantasy 106
fault 40, 56
fear 85
feelings 82, 84, 122
    internalising feelings 104
    trusting feelings 58
fetishism 79
filth 27
flasher 34
fondling 91
'forgiveness' 95
gambling 27, 28, 53, 65
Garston 30
'good girl' 28
Gracewell Clinic 13, 17, 53, 89
    'House of Loathing' 64
grandfather 13, 27–30, 46, 53, 122
    death of 33
grief 33
grooming 13, 66, 75, 100
guilt 28, 33, 49
guitar 32, 106
harm
    minimising harm 17
Harper, Sarah 77
hatred 87
healing 113, 122
Hemel Hempstead 13, 43
Hogg, Caroline 77
Holy Rood school 30
Home Office 90
horror 58

horseplay *101*
Horsfield, John *14*
Houghton Regis (man from) *40*
humiliation *104*, *119*, *125*
ignorance *76*, *90*
image *44*
inhibitors *83*
insignificance *104*
instincts *122*
integrity *64*, *78*
invisibility *63*
Isle of Wight *52*
isolation *102*
Jane *33*, *84*, *103–107*
jealousy *86*
Joe (father) *21*, *27*, *47*
Kew Gardens *40*
Kidscape *13*
kindness *23*, *79*
knee-jerk reactions, solutions, etc. *viii*, *76*
knowledge *87*
  sexual knowledge *35*
language *viii*, *14*, *58*, *71–73*, *80*, *100*, *109–128*
  'accurate' language *124*
  inner rescuing language *121*
Las Vegas *65*
learned behaviour *119*
Letchworth Mental Health Unit *56*
lewd, etc. behaviour *80*
listening *75*
Lister Hospital *56*
locked-outness *29*
logic *123*

loitering *93*
love *28*, *59*, *79*, *105*
Lucy *73*, *132*, *135*
Luton *43*
  Luton Rape Crisis Centre *v*, *55*, *71*
marriage *42*, *59*
Martin *87*
Mary (mother) *21*
mask *45*, *107*
Maureen *103–107*
Maxwell, Susan *77*
Mazlish, Elaine *110*
media *75*
metacognition *120*
Michael *123*
Milton Keynes *135*
minimising *57*, *58*, *80*
mocking *119*
modesty *110*
monsters *18*, *86*
'Mr Creepy' *72*
murder *78*
  Murder of Childhood *v*, *14*, *75*
music *32*, *106*
narrow-mindedness *64*
National Society for the Prevention of Cruelty to Children *14*
negative messages, etc. *26*, *37*, *38*, *41*, *100*, *110*
neglect *57*
nimbyism *17*, *90*
normalising *17*, *27*
nothingness *32*
nuns *30*
'one-off' offences *82*, *94*

paedophilia *vii, 93*
pain *107*
parents *27, 49, 57*
personality *81*
perverts *89*
Peskett, Ange *32, 106*
Pete *42, 55*
Peterhead Prison *65*
pillars of society *99*
poker *65*
politeness *21, 28, 34, 114*
pornography *73, 101*
power *29, 127*
   power struggle *64*
predator *17*
prejudice *90*
pretending *82, 107*
Price, Trevor *17, 64–65*
priests *94*
probation *17, 65*
   Probation Service *52, 81*
   volunteer *52*
promiscuity *31*
prostitution *31*
protection *104*
psychology *17, 60–61, 109*
psychopaths *64*
public opinion *vii*
rape *56, 97, 106, 125*
reality *22, 38, 106, 121*
red-herrings *99*
Red House *79*
referrals *17*
rejection *85, 119*
re-offending *90*

rescue *76, 122*
respect *21, 110*
responsibility *17, 43, 80, 95*
revulsion *86*
risk *90*
role models *79*
Royal Navy *51*
rudeness *119*
ruses *100*
ruthlessness *65*
Sadie *24*
safety *vi, 28, 114*
   familiarity and safety *125*
sailor *52*
'Sally' *98*
sarcasm *119*
Saughton Prison *65*
school *22, 25, 28*
scolding *119*
Scotland *77, 132*
scrutiny
   public scrutiny *89*
Sean *117*
secrets *45, 101, 104, 121, 122*
seediness *30, 52*
self-confidence *37, 111*
self-delusion *81*
self-esteem *26, 63, 107*
self-harm *33, 56, 104*
self-hate *30*
self-help *123*
   self-help group *13, 46*
self-worth *26, 41, 104*
sentencing *65*
sex *31*

Pick-up the Pieces

as a weapon *33, 105*
  derailed attitude to *107*
  sex-offenders *17, 52, 64, 89*
  sexual knowledge *35*
shock *28, 58, 103, 131*
silence *34, 91, 95, 98, 102*
Sister Frances *32*
solace *106*
stalking *40*
stereotyping *23, 58*
Surrey *17*
survival *46, 96, 106*
sympathy *58*
targeting *13, 48, 66, 75*
Tate, Genette *77*
teachers *28–30*
telling *104*
terror *77*
therapy *38, 53, 76*
  group therapy *91*
Thornhill, Teresa *82–84*
time-out *119, 129*
touching *91, 127*
trauma *79, 121*
treatment *76*
trust *72, 91*
  positions of trust *95*
  self-trust *112*
Tulip, Jack and Margaret *78*
Turner, Laura *82*
'uncomfortable' *81, 117, 123*
understanding *58, 76, 90*
upbringing *78, 107, 115*
utopia *21, 27*
Uxbridge *34*

victims *vii, 34, 55, 76, 102, 103–107*
Vincent, Sally *64*
voices *37–39, 38*
vulnerability *48, 114*
Watford *30*
Willie, Uncle *23*
Woburn Sands *56*
Wolvercote Clinic *17*
words *109, 120, 127*
Wyre, Ray *v, vii, 13, 51–54, 59–70*
  chaotic *68*
  charisma *59, 129*
  Christian faith *52*
  generosity *59*
Zeedyk, Suzanne *120*

NEW TWENTY-FIFTH ANNIVERSARY EDITION

The Murder of Childhood
Inside the Mind of One of Britain's Most Notorious Child Murderers
Ray Wyre and Tim Tate
With Charmaine Richardson

Contains extracts from Ray Wyre's revealing interviews with child serial-killer Robert Black. Tim Tate and Charmaine Richardson (Wyre's widow) have meticulously re-visited a work out of print for a decade, adding a fresh Introduction, Preface, Index and endpiece, 'Twenty-five Years Later ....'

They show how events have changed, including the further conviction of child serial-killer Robert Black for the murder of Jennifer Cardy and developments in policing methods, but criticise a continuing, possibly worse, failure to protect children from paedophiles in the internet age. They voice real concern that Ray Wyre's call to learn more about sex-offenders, their methods of operation and strategies of denial, distortion, deflection of blame and need for treatment, have gone unheeded. Ultimately, the book paints a picture of political regression.

Paperback & ebook | ISBN 978-1-909976-62-7 | 2nd Edn. | 2018 | 306 pages

www.WatersidePress.co.uk

www.ingramcontent.com/pod-product-compliance
Lightning Source LLC
Chambersburg PA
CBHW020100170426
43199CB00009B/344